SO SEND I YOU

A STUDY IN PERSONAL
SOUL WINNING

Jointly Authored by

RALPH M. RIGGS
WILDON COLBAUGH
D. V. HURST
BURTON PIERCE
STANTON JOHNSON
ROBERT L. BRANDT

GOSPEL PUBLISHING HOUSE
Springfield, Missouri 65802
2-587

FOREWORD

Without doubt, the church needs to "go!" Believers need to get involved everywhere in soul-winning encounters. *So Send I You* is a Bible anchored appeal for such involvement. R. M. Riggs, the author of the first four chapters, forcefully recounts the simplicity and comprehensiveness of God's plan of redemption. With impact he sets the strategic place each disciple of Christ occupies in the plan and in its propagation.

The book is heavily Bible-based, containing over two hundred Scripture references. Carefully documented is Jesus' example in reaching men and women in homes, in places of business and on the street. The clear implication is that this is God's way today. He notes the key verbs—*go, witness, teach,* and *preach,* with the emphasis on the whole world as the field.

Bible commands are translated into "work-a-day" action. The author not only strongly appeals for full involvement on the part of all disciples, but sets forth practical ways whereby they can be involved.

There is no one in Pentecostal circles today more eminently qualified to state the case for soul winning than Ralph M. Riggs. The principles set forth in this book have been a "way of life" for Brother Riggs through fifty years of fruitful and effectual ministry as a writer, teacher, pastor, missionary, and church administrator.

The Biblical foundations laid by R. M. Riggs are followed by a careful study of ways to reach people for Christ. Wildon Colbaugh, promotions coordinator for REVIVALTIME, discusses the subject "Ways of Witnessing." He tells where we will find people and how we can reach them. He notes nineteen places you can find prospects and helps clarify what kind of visit is needed most.

In chapters 6, 7, and 8 Christians will learn how to guide the conversation rather than merely waiting for ideal opportunities to come. The "approach" to a soul-winning conversation is discussed by D. V. Hurst, co-ordinator of the Spiritual Life—Evangelism Commission. After showing how to get started, he turns to the very important subject of making a "transition" to the subject of salvation.

Once Christians have reached this point in conversation they frequently wonder, "What do I say now?" Burton Pierce, secretary of the Men's Fellowship Department, gives them the answer. He deals with the "conversation" itself. Not just a formula, this chapter guides the Christian in knowing how to move with the Spirit, drawing the prospect closer and closer to a decision in favor of Christ.

Stanton Johnson, pastor, Ottumwa, Iowa, concludes the "conversation" by showing how to bring it to a close that includes the person's decision to accept Christ. He also deals with the subject of helping the person gain assurance in his new faith.

The final chapter of *So Send I You,* written by R. L. Brandt, secretary of the Home Missions Department, deals with helping the new Christian become established in the church, strengthening him, and helping him assume Christian service as he matures in his experience.

So Send I You is welcomed as a valuable and timely addition to the evangelism thrust being made by the Assemblies of God today. It will enrich and inspire the lives of all those who read it.

THOS. F. ZIMMERMAN
General Superintendent

CONTENTS

PREFACE

Christ's ministry to the earth did not stop with His death. Just before He died and returned to His Father, He twice left instructions about continuing His ministry on earth. He intended to do this through his disciples.

In His high-priestly prayer, Christ declared to His Father (in the hearing of His disciples), "As thou hast sent me into the world, even so have I also sent them into the world."[1] On the first night after His resurrection, Jesus stated directly to His disciples, "As my Father hath sent me, even so send I you."[2] With the words "So send I you," Jesus projected His ministry into and through the work of His disciples. This is the plan of redemption and the Great Commission in a nutshell.

News of a Saviour has been heralded to many nations and people. Revival campaigns in local churches and city-wide crusades; local, national, and international radio broadcasts and telecasts; gospel literature distribution—all are being pushed forward diligently. "Yet there is room."[3] There are still many who have not responded, many who have not even heard.

The time has come for the church to employ its best means of spreading the gospel. This is the method used by Jesus and His disciples and the Christians of the Apostolic Age. Those disciples had no radio or television, no printing presses, no airplanes, no steamboats or automobiles; yet they permeated the then-known world with the gospel message.

What method had been followed? These verses sum it up for us. "Daily in the temple, and in every house, they ceased not to teach and preach Jesus Christ."[4] "I . . . have shewed you, and have taught you publicly, and from house to house."[5]

Each local congregation, under the leadership of its pastor, should go from house to house, not merely to invite people to church or take a census of the neighborhood, but to present Christ as Lord and Saviour. Personal house-to-house soul winning is the need of the hour. It is our last hope and the world's last chance. It worked in those early days. It will succeed in our day. It is still Christ's plan and His command. "Go ye into all the world, and preach the gospel to every creature."[6]

We must get out of our comfortable churches and go into the highways and hedges. We must be witnesses unto Him "both in Jerusalem, and in all Judea, and in Samaria, and unto the uttermost part of the earth."[7] The early disciples obeyed Him. We must give this gospel method a chance. We must give our neighbor and the world an earnest personal invitation to accept Christ.

When Spirit-filled people have the courage and the faithfulness to obey our Lord and follow the apostolic pattern in spreading the true gospel, we will see the whole world evangelized in this generation.

CHAPTER 1

REDEMPTION—THE BASIS FOR WINNING SOULS

The most important business ever transacted was Jesus' purchase of the world. The price He paid was His life. The world belonged to God by creation, but it had lost God's fellowship because of the deliberate rebellion of His creatures. Men chose to become the followers of Satan, and the ungodly usurped leadership over the world.

PURCHASING REDEMPTION THROUGH CHRIST

This loss was grievous in the sight of God, so He put into action His plan of redemption, conceived before the foundations of the world. He would buy back His creation at a price commensurate to its value. "I wept much, because no man was found worthy . . . one of the elders saith unto me, Weep not: Behold the Lion of the tribe of Judah, the Root of David, hath prevailed."[1] So the Lord Jesus Christ, the Son of almighty God, gave His life in redemption of the world. It was a price not only commensurate with, but far in excess of, the value of the world.

A SUFFICIENT PRICE

Nothing less than this complete provision would be consistent with the magnitude of God's wealth and power. It befitted God to pay ample price for the redemption of the world.

When this Redeemer arrived on the banks of Jordan, John the Baptist declared, "Behold the Lamb of God, which taketh away the sin of the world."[2] The sin of *the world* was taken away when this Lamb was sacrificed on Calvary. When John the Apostle was writing to his "little children," he declared, "If any man sin, we have an advocate with the Father, Jesus Christ the righteous: and He is the propitiation for our sins: and not for ours only, but also for the sins of the whole world."[3] In Paul's first letter to Timothy, he referred to Christ, "who gave himself a ransom for all" and "who is the Saviour of all men, specially of those that believe."[4] There was no limit to this atonement. He redeemed the world, the whole world, all men!

This was, indeed, ample price to pay. Infinitely more was sacrificed than was effectively redeemed, even though the entire world was purchased. Colossians 1:16 declares, "By him were all things created, that are in heaven, and that are in earth." John 1:3 states, "All things were made by him; and without him was not anything made that was made." Jesus Christ the Creator gave His life to redeem the world. Who can deny that the Creator is worth more than His creatures?

A WORTHY PRICE

This infinite Creator sacrificed His very life for the redemption of the earth and its inhabitants. How unspeakably sufficient was the atonement thus made. God so loved the world—the whole world, all men— that He gave His Son that whosoever—no matter how many they may be—who believe in Him, could be redeemed from the perishing to which they were otherwise doomed. It is no wonder heaven breaks forth in a new song, saying, "Thou art worthy . . . for thou wast slain, and hast redeemed us to God by thy blood out of every kindred, and tongue, and people, and nation. . . . And . . . many angels round about the throne . . . saying with a loud voice, Worthy is the Lamb that was slain. . . . And every creature which is in heaven, and on the earth, and under the earth, and such as are in the sea, and all that are in them, heard I saying, Blessing and honour, and glory, and power, be unto him that sitteth upon the throne, and unto the Lamb forever and ever."[5]

PROVIDING REDEMPTION FOR ALL

Could anyone imagine that the God, who gave His only begotten Son in death to redeem all the world, would not desire that all men should be saved? If there is any question about it, His Word tells us plainly that He does want every man to be saved. Note these verses. It is God who "will have all men to be saved, and to come unto the knowledge of the truth."[6] It is the Lord who is "longsuffering to usward, not willing that any should perish, but that all should come to repentance."[7] Here is a double statement, one negative and the other positive to the same effect: He does not want anyone to perish, and He does want all to be saved. Christ Himself in John 3:17 declared, "God sent not his Son into the world to condemn the world; but that the world through him might be saved." Could anything be clearer? His death was the most eloquent declaration; His words, many times repeated, tell us plainly that the purpose of His death was to redeem the whole world.

ALL MUST HEAR OF REDEMPTION

When Jesus sent His disciples to proclaim redemption to all the world, He specifically declared that it should be to all nations, to every creature. "Go ye therefore, and teach all nations."[8] "Go ye into all the world, and preach the gospel to every creature."[9] "Repentance and remission of sins should be preached in his name among all nations, beginning at Jerusalem."[10]

Since all were purchased by His blood and since He wants every man to be saved, Jesus therefore commanded His messengers to declare the news of the forgiveness of sins and potential redemption to every creature on earth. The Bible specifically declares that He is no respector of persons.[11] Also the Scripture says, "Whosoever believeth on him shall not be ashamed. For there is no difference between the Jew and the Greek: for the same Lord over all is rich unto all that call upon him. For whosoever shall call upon the name of the Lord shall be saved."[12]

What shall we say to these things? The whole world is purchased by Christ's blood, and God wants the whole world to be saved. He has commanded that every creature shall be told of this redemption. There is absolutely no distinction in the value of men in the matter of their souls' salvation. Does it follow then that all men will, therefore, automatically be saved?

MEN MUST ACCEPT REDEMPTION

Mark 16:15 is followed by this statement, "He that believeth and is baptized shall be saved; but he that believeth not shall be damned." Here is a division of humanity. All were purchased. God wants all to be saved. He wants us to preach to every creature. But these creatures to whom we preach and this world for whom the full price of redemption is paid, consists of individuals who, one by one, are free moral agents. "Whosoever will, let him take of the water of life freely."[13]

The Great Commission specifically declares that all those who will not accept the gospel will be damned. After John 3:16, Jesus says, "He that believeth on him is not condemned: but he that believeth not is condemned already."[14] And, "He that believeth on the Son hath everlasting life: and he that believeth not the Son shall not see life; but the wrath of God abideth on him."[15]

Here we have the awful story that when the gospel is preached to all the world, there shall be a division among the people of the world. A number will be saved, thank God. There will be those who will believe the gospel. They will not be condemned. They will have everlasting life. But over against that happy company, there will be those who will not believe. Those who do not believe will not see life; the wrath of God will abide upon them. Jesus will come "in flaming fire taking vengeance on them that know not God and that obey not the gospel of our Lord Jesus Christ."[16] This could refer to those who deliberately reject the gospel and also to those who for any reason do not know God. These verses also are in the Bible and must be believed.

TELLING THE WORLD OF REDEMPTION

When Jacob fled from his brother Esau, "he lighted upon a certain place, and tarried there all night, . . . and lay down in that place to sleep. And he dreamed, and behold a ladder set up on the earth, and the top of it reached to heaven: and behold the angels of God ascending and descending on it."[17] Jesus told Nathaniel, "Verily, verily, I say unto you, Hereafter ye shall see heaven open, and the angels of God ascending and descending upon the Son of man."[18] Both passages tell of angels of God ascending and descending between earth and heaven. Jacob saw a ladder connecting earth and heaven, and Jesus implied that He, that is, His work, would be that Ladder.

The interpretation of this dream and figure of speech is not hard to find. Heaven will be opened. There will be found a way from earth to heaven. Christ is that Way. The redemption He made possible has established communion between earth and heaven. Men can ascend to heaven by accepting redemption through Christ. God's blessing descends from heaven upon those who are redeemed.

THE WORK OF THE FATHER

Luke 24:46-48 tells us about the rungs in Salvation's Ladder. The work of Father, Son, and Holy Spirit constitute the three upper rungs. The Father's part was to love the world and to give His Son, to sanctify His Son and send His Son into the world.[19] "God was in Christ, reconciling the world unto Himself" through Christ's death and resurrection.[20]

THE WORK OF THE SON

The Son's part was to give His life a ransom. "His own self bare our sins in his own body on the tree."[21] "I lay down my life for the sheep. . . . No man taketh it from me, but I lay it down of myself."[22] "It behooved Christ to suffer," and He did.[23]

THE WORK OF THE HOLY SPIRIT

The part which the Holy Spirit plays is twofold. In the first place, it is He who convicts men of sin and draws them to God. "When he is come, he will reprove the world of sin."[24] "No man can come to me, except the Father which hath sent me draw him."[25] This the Father does through the Holy Spirit. "And I, if I be lifted up from the earth, will draw all men unto me."[26] This drawing is done by the Holy Spirit.

In the second place, it is the Holy Spirit who anoints the disciples with power to enable them to witness for Christ. "Ye shall receive power, after that the Holy Ghost is come upon you: and ye shall be witnesses unto me."[27] Thus the Father, the Son, and the Holy Ghost have given themselves to constitute part of the ladder from earth to heaven.

THE WORK OF THE DISCIPLES

Is this all? Is there not still another rung in Salvation's Ladder? The Bible tells us that there is at least one more. It is constituted by the work of disciples of our Lord: the disciples then and the disciples now.

When Luke said, "It behoved Christ to suffer, and to rise from the dead," he extended his statement to include the results of Christ's work, namely, "that repentance and remission of sins should be preached. . . . And ye are witnesses of these things."[28] In other words, it behoved the disciples to preach, just as it behoved Christ to suffer and the Father to raise Him from the dead. Thus there are four rungs in this ladder: the work of Father, Son, Holy Spirit, and the disciples who were to witness and to preach.

"How then shall they call on him in whom they have not believed? and how shall they believe in him of whom they have not heard? and how shall they hear without a preacher?"[29] How can they reach the third rung without the fourth to stand on? After Christ paid the price for the redemption of the world, He sent His disciples into all the world to tell the story. "Go ye therefore."[30] When the Lord effected the salvation of Cornelius, He employed an angel, not to tell the story of salvation, but to tell Cornelius to call for Peter who would tell him that story.[31] He does not entrust angels with the task of telling salvation's story; He uses His disciples for that purpose. It was they who were anointed to preach.

1. *All disciples share in this work.* Those immediate disciples, being only twelve in number, could not possibly go into all the world. It was physically impossible. And they would not live long enough. Obviously, they could not be the only persons used to reach all generations until the end of the age. It follows, therefore, that God's plan for proclaiming the gospel was merely launched by those first disciples and that the Lord intended successive generations of disciples to witness to their own respective generations. "The things that thou hast heard of me among many witnesses, the same commit thou to faithful men, who shall be able to teach others also."[32] In His high-priestly prayer, Christ specifically included those "also which shall believe on me through their word."[33] He included us in His prayer and in the plan of redemption.

2. *All converts learn to share in this work.* In the Great Commission according to Matthew, the Lord specifically stated that when disciples were made they

should be told to observe all things which He had commanded the first disciples. This transfers to all succeeding converts His command to go and preach the gospel to every creature. When He said, according to Mark 16:15-17, "Go ye into all the world, and preach the gospel to every creature. He that believeth and is baptized shall be saved; ... And these signs shall follow them that believe," He bequeathed to the new believers His divine power to cast out devils, lay hands on the sick, and in every way carry on the ministry of the gospel. Thus, not alone to these first preachers, but to those also who became believers as a result of their preaching, should be given partnership in gospel propagation.

We cannot escape the conclusion that all His disciples are a rung in Salvation's Ladder. It is also true that the disciples constitute the rung which is closest to the earth, the very first rung by which men are to climb upward toward heaven. If that first rung is broken or fails to function as such, what happens to the multitudes dependent on it? How vital indeed, then, is the function and ministry of all Christ's children, His true disciples. Philip Hogan, foreign missions director of the Assemblies of God, describes the Great Commission in these words: "The Great Commission is God-given, man-conducted; Christ-purchased, man-propagated; Holy Spirit empowered, humanly endeavored; ushering in the day when the kingdoms of this world shall become the Kingdom of our God and His Christ."

CHAPTER **2**

PATTERNS OF SOUL WINNING

A common characteristic of the new Christian is a burning desire to share this experience with others. This is, of course, as it should be. But then comes the question, "How do I go about it?" We learn many things through the examples of others; winning souls is no exception. Let us turn our attention in this chapter to examples God Himself has set for us through the work of the Father and Jesus Christ the Son.

GOD, THE FIRST EXAMPLE

God the Father loved the world, and gave His Son to redeem it. But that was not all. None other than God the Father set an example for us by seeking to save the lost.

GOD SOUGHT ADAM

God gave us the first example of soul winning when He dealt with Adam and Eve after their fall. They had sinned and were in trouble. But they were not seeking God. Rather, they were hiding from Him. Then, "they heard the voice of the Lord God walking in the garden in the cool of the day: . . . and the Lord God called unto Adam, and said unto him, Where art thou?"[1] This is a perfect pattern for soul-winning evangelism.

10

Mankind today is in trouble, but he is not seeking God; he is hiding from God.

God has the same attitude toward men today that He had toward the first man; He comes down to find man and to engage him in conversation to uncover his need. Then, as with Adam, God reveals to man the solution to his troubles.

This is the example God has set for us. Now we are responsible for finding those who are hiding from God; and we must, by skillful conversation, uncover their needs and reveal to them the solution to their troubles by introducing them to the Great Redeemer.

GOD SOUGHT TO SAVE LOT AND SODOM

What applied to one man and his wife in the Garden of Eden applied to a city in the time of Abraham. The Lord appeared to Abraham as he sat in his tent door in the heat of the day.[2] He informed Abraham of the approaching birth of a son in fulfillment of His promise of a Redeemer in his lineage. God also told Abraham of the judgment soon to come upon Sodom and Gomorrah. Although the cities were sinful enough to deserve immediate and complete destruction, the Lord detoured on His way to effect that destruction in order to give Abraham a chance to intercede on their behalf.

Lot was living in Sodom. Abraham was interested primarily in Lot, but the Lord was willing to save the entire city in response to Abraham's pleading. God is "merciful and gracious, longsuffering and abundant in goodness and truth, keeping mercy for thousands, forgiving iniquity and transgression and sin."[3] God proved His mercy by personally honoring the intercession of Abraham. Our Father again came to seek

and to save that which was lost, and He left an example for us to follow.

GOD SOUGHT TO SAVE THE ISRAELITES

The next picture of the Father is in His response
to the need of an entire nation. He found Abraham
in the heat of the day in the tent door. Now, on the
backside of a desert, God found a humble herdsman
tending his sheep. He created the phenomenon of a
burning bush that was not consumed to attract Moses'
attention.[4] When Moses turned aside to look, the Lord
said to him, "Behold, the cry of the children of Israel
is come unto me: and I have also seen the oppression
wherewith the Egyptians oppress them."[5]

Here is another example of God's determination to
help in need. He performed miracles before Moses;
and later, through Moses, before Pharaoh. There are
no lengths to which He will not go to bring deliver-
ance.

GOD USED SAMUEL AS A MESSENGER

Many centuries later this nation of Israel, safely
established in the land of Canaan, had departed from
serving God. But God could not let it remain so.
Once more He sought an instrument through which
He could bring a message to the people whom He
loved, even though they were so wayward. This time
He chose to use a little boy, Samuel. "Now Samuel
did not yet know the Lord, neither was the word of
the Lord yet revealed unto him."[6] One night when
Samuel lay down to sleep, the Lord called to him.
The lad ran to Eli the priest, thinking it was he who
had called him. Eli explained that it was not he and
sent Samuel back to lie down again. Three times God
called Samuel until, under the coaching of Eli, Samuel

learned to respond. Then God gave him a message concerning the house of Eli and the nation of Israel.

GOD USED ISAIAH AS A PROPHET

Hundreds of years passed and a king of Judah died. Faithfully the Lord revealed Himself to His servant Isaiah. "Whom shall I send, and who will go for us?"[7] God was seeking someone through whom He could help that needy nation. The consistent, persistent Heavenly Father was still seeking to save that which was lost. He did not wait for them to come to Him; He sought them even while they still rebelled against Him. Once again He gave us an example in His own actions.

GOD SENT HIS SON AS THE REDEEMER

The grand climax of the examples God has set for us is stated in John 1:14. Not a voice, as to Adam in the cool of the day; nor an angel of the Lord, as to Abraham in the heat of the day; nor a voice in a burning bush, as to Moses on the backside of the desert; nor even a call in the night, as to the little boy Samuel —this time God sent His only begotten Son in the likeness of sinful flesh to make a long, persistent, earnest appeal to the sons of men to accept His salvation. "The Word was made flesh, and dwelt among us."[8] "No man hath seen God at any time; the only begotten Son, which is in the bosom of the Father, he hath declared him."[9] Thus the Father was in the Son as He walked the hills of Judea and the plains of Galilee and went throughout every city and village seeking to save that which was lost.

THE FATHER SET A CLEAR EXAMPLE

From Genesis 3 and Revelation 3, we have the same

picture, "Behold I stand at the door, and knock." God is still doing house-to-house visitation, ringing doorbells, knocking, and calling, "If any man hear my voice—"[10] What a perfect example our Heavenly Father has set before us. Oh, that we may be the children of our Father which is in heaven!

CHRIST, THE SECOND EXAMPLE

We turn now to an examination of the example set for us by Christ our Lord. He, like His Father, teaches us by divine example how to win the souls of men.

CHRIST USED HIS HOME TO WIN HIS FIRST DISCIPLES

After Christ's baptism by John and His temptation in the wilderness, He returned to Jordan. John the Baptist witnessed concerning Him saying, "Behold the Lamb of God, which taketh away the sin of the world. . . . Again the next day after John stood, and two of his disciples; and looking upon Jesus as he walked, he saith, Behold the Lamb of God!"[11] Whereupon, the two disciples turned to follow Jesus. Jesus saw them following and invited them to come and see where He dwelt. These disciples were Andrew, Simon Peter's brother, and (it is assumed) John, who became the beloved disciple. These two "abode with Him that day," since it was about four o'clock in the afternoon. The conversation was long and intimate and resulted in their becoming His devout disciples. How easy this was for Jesus. His Father had prepared the way for His first experience of winning people to Himself. He simply carried out the plan which was so evidently His Father's will. The first disciples, then, were won in spiritual conversation in Christ's own home.

CHRIST WAS LED BY THE SPIRIT TO PHILIP AND NATHANIEL

The next convert was Philip. "The day following
Jesus would go forth into Galilee, and findeth Philip,
and saith unto him, Follow me."[15] It was discernment on the part of Christ and direct leading in His
own heart which enabled Him to find Philip, extend-
ing to him an invitation to become His disciple. Nathaniel was soon added. This too is a bona fide way
of doing personal evangelism: responding to the
prompting and leading of the spirit in one's own
heart in choosing persons with whom we should speak
concerning salvation.

CHRIST WON NICODEMUS PERSONALLY

After His disciples had followed Him to Capernaum,
they went down with Him to the Passover Feast at
Jerusalem. Here Nicodemus came to talk with Jesus.
With Nicodemus it was strictly a case of "the fish
jumping into the boat." John tells us that Nicodemus
sought out Jesus at night and engaged Him in spiritual conversation. How fortunate we are to have that
discourse preserved for us. To this one man, the Lord
poured out a torrent of profound spiritual truth which
has provided ample sermon material for many generations! "Ye must be born again." "That which is born
of the Spirit is spirit." The Holy Spirit is like the
wind that blows. Jesus will be lifted up as Moses lifted
up the serpent in the wilderness. And then the most
well-known text of the Bible.[13] Jesus won him quickly
by the patient attention which He gave him as recorded in John 3.

CHRIST SOUGHT THE WOMAN OF SAMARIA

"After these things came Jesus and his disciples into
the land of Judea; and there he tarried with them,

and baptized. . . . (Though Jesus himself baptized not,
but his disciples,) He left Judea, and departed again
into Galilee. And he must needs go through Samaria."[14] Here, apparently quite casually and naturally,
Christ led a woman to accept Him as the Messiah.
Each step was clearly depicted. He came to a certain
city as He traveled. Being weary with the journey,
He sat on the well while His disciples went away into
the city to buy food. As He sat there, a woman from
the village came to draw water. A very normal, natural
event; and it followed easily that the Lord would ask
her for a drink of water, since apparently there was
no public provision for drawing water. Jesus began
immediately to converse with the woman in a way
which would lead her to an acknowledgment of Himself as the Messiah. The conversation is written out
in John 4 in order that we all may read how Jesus
"led a soul to Christ."

1. *He ignored social distinctions.* The very fact that
Jesus spoke to this Samaritan woman began to break
down the social barriers and establish a friendly cli-
mate. His opening remark was a simple, easy request
for a drink of water. This began the conversation on
a casual subject. She was astonished, and her immediate response was, "How is it that thou, being a Jew,
askest drink of me, which am a woman of Samaria."[15]
There was a social gap between the Jews and the
Samaritans of which she was very conscious but which
Jesus deliberately ignored or bridged. This means
there should be no social aloofness maintained by any
personal worker. With all the various strata of society
which exist today, this ought to be a pointed and
practical lesson to us. She was not only a Samaritan
but a woman of bad reputation. This widened the

social gap, but it did not make the gap too wide for our Lord to span. Her soul was worth far more than any social propriety (which is really social pride), so Jesus immediately ignored all hindrances and engaged her in conversation.

2. *He used a point of contact.* Although Jesus was still thirsty for natural water, He was more interested in bringing spiritual blessing to this woman. He used the conversation about water as an illustration of the spiritual blessing that He stood ready to give to her. When she heard that He had water that could be more satisfying than the water she had, she asked Jesus to give her that water. Thus He was following the well-known pedagogical law of using the known to introduce the unknown. She knew what water was, how it satisfied, and how very necessary it was. It seemed easy to understand that He had a spiritual blessing that would satisfy, and this was very important to her. He couched His words so as to identify Himself with the living water.

3. *He made salvation personal.* Nearly everyone is willing to talk about religion; it is a general subject. But Christ would not let it remain general. He pointed out personal need and personal benefit. He brought the woman face to face with the record of her own life. He moved from a comment on habits of worship to the requirement of personal relationship with God. The soul winner must bring his conversation to the point of personal salvation and individual need.

4. *He faced the question of sin.* There is a tendency in modern Christianity to exhort people merely to "follow Jesus." Many preachers ignore the question of repentance of sin and the redemption which Christ purchased at such infinite cost at Calvary. Our Lord

did not follow this tactic. He did not ignore the woman's sins, nor would He let her do so. The sin question had to be faced and settled. Tactfully the Lord used her reference to having no husband to call attention to the fact that she had had five husbands, and the man with whom she now lived was not her husband. What a charge and what a condition of sin! She did not deny this charge, but she recognized in Him One who knew all about her. Later she reported to the men of the city, "Come, see a man, which told me all things that ever I did." In her acknowledgment of sin there came into her heart and mind a greater appreciation of Him with whom she spoke. "Sir, I perceive that thou art a prophet." This was real progress: from a tacit acknowledgment of sin, she moved toward an acknowledgment of a Saviour.

5. *He avoided controversy.* Human nature always tends toward self-defense and escape. The Samaritan woman sought to escape by engaging Jesus in controversy. "The Samaritans worship in the Samaritan mountain, but the Jews worship in Jerusalem," she said. In other words, "Which church is right? We think ours is right for us, although Jerusalem may be right for you." Jesus refused to be diverted from His goal. He turned her comment into an explanation of His Father who taught people to worship Him anywhere and everywhere, in spirit and in truth. This brought on her reference to the Messiah, the Christ. "When he is come, he will tell us all things." This is the point to which He was seeking to bring her, so He was ready to announce, "I that speak unto thee am He." She accepted this statement and went immediately to tell others that she had found Him who was the Christ. This is the climax of all soul winning

(to believe and then to begin to tell others), and it is the conclusion of the record of the most perfect case of soul winning ever known.

CHRIST USED SIMON'S HOUSE AS A BASE OF BLESSING

Christ then went on through Samaria into Galilee and again to Capernaum where He taught in the synagogue. He "arose out of the synagogue, and entered into Simon's house. And Simon's wife's mother was taken with a great fever; and they besought him for her. And He stood over her, and rebuked the fever; and it left her: and immediately she arose and ministered unto them."[16] This aroused faith so that during the evening all those who had sick friends and relatives brought them unto Him; and He laid His hands on everyone of them and healed them.[17] Thus again He made a private home the scene of a wonderful miracle which stimulated the neighbors and led to many healings.

CHRIST WON MATTHEW AND TAUGHT IN HIS HOUSE

Sometime after this Jesus went forth "and saw a publican, named Levi, sitting at the receipt of custom: and he said unto him, Follow me. And he left all, rose up, and followed him. And Levi made him a great feast in his own house: and there was a great company of publicans and of others that sat down with them."[18] On this occasion Jesus went to a man as he was busy at his secular occupation and extended to him a personal invitation to become His disciple. Later Jesus went into a person's home and ministered to a company of people assembled there.

CHRIST MINISTERED IN A PHARISEE'S HOUSE

Not long after this "one of the Pharisees desired

him that he would eat with him. And he went into
the Pharisee's house, and sat down to meat."[19] This
time Jesus chose the home of one of His enemies. He
would go into anyone's home where He would have
an opportunity to minister to those in need. It was
not the Pharisee, however, who believed on Him this
time. It was a woman, a sinful woman, who came with
an alabaster box of ointment to anoint Him. In response to the unspoken criticism of her act by the
Pharisee, Jesus told the story of the two debtors. He
concluded by telling the woman that her sins were
forgiven. This too drew the criticism of the Pharisee
and his friends who sat at meat with Him. But Jesus
was again using a private home as a pulpit from which
to teach and forgive sins.

CHRIST TAUGHT IN MARTHA'S HOUSE

In the ministry of our Lord in Judea, the home of
Martha and Mary and Lazarus was open to Him,
doubtless as a resting place. Into this home in Bethany,
Jesus came one day as Martha was preparing a meal.
Mary took advantage of His presence to sit at His
feet and hear the wonderful words that fell from His
lips. Who of us can forget His words when He said
that Mary had chosen the good part and that it was
not good to be cumbered about many things! This
home also became remembered both as a place of
entertainment of the Christ and a place where some
of His beautiful ministry was performed.

CHRIST WON ZACCHAEUS IN HIS HOME

In Luke 19, as Jesus approached the end of His
ministry, we find another time when He went into a
private home. This time it was the home of Zacchaeus,
a despised tax collector. Zacchaeus had climbed a syca-

more tree to get a better look at Jesus. At the same
time, Jesus not only saw Zacchaeus, but He saw into
Zacchaeus' heart. He knew this was a man who would
accept Him. He called to Zacchaeus to come down
and announced that He was going home with him
that day. Here Jesus took the initiative in winning a
soul. He actually invited Himself into a man's home
and even into the home of a man who was a despised
publican and a sinner. There was no home so "off-
bounds" that Jesus would not enter it in His quest
for souls. He forgave the sins of Zacchaeus and announced that salvation had come to that home. There
He made this immortal announcement, "For the Son
of Man is come to seek and to save that which was
lost."[20]

CHRIST WON THE MAN AT THE POOL OF BETHESDA

Another example of Christ's soul winning is the case
of the man at the pool of Bethesda. Again our Lord
took the initiative. He found a certain man whom He
discerned was ready for His ministry. He said to the
man, "Wilt thou be made whole?"[21] Jesus healed him
even though it was the sabbath day and despite the
fact that it would precipitate an argument with the
Jews. Later He found this man in the temple and
revealed Himself to him.

CHRIST WON MEN AT THEIR PLACES OF BUSINESS

Jesus did not hesitate to find people at their places
of business. On His visit to Capernaum where He
had ministered in Peter's home, He went down to the
Sea of Galilee and there extended a personal, permanent call to Simon Peter and his brother, and to James
and John, the sons of Zebedee. He had had fellowship with them for some months, but now it was time

for them to leave all and become His permanent followers. As with Matthew later on, He sought and found them at their place of business. So Jesus entered homes and places of business to teach and preach, to heal and forgive sins, and to call people to become His disciples.

CHRIST SET A CLEAR EXAMPLE

There are sweeping general statements in Scripture to show that this approach to winning men was Jesus' habit. "Jesus went about all the cities and villages, teaching in their synagogues, and preaching the gospel of the kingdom, and healing every sickness and every disease among the people."[22] "And it came to pass afterward, that He went throughout every city and village, preaching and shewing the glad tidings of the kingdom of God: and the twelve were with Him."[23] He not only taught glad tidings, but He demonstrated (showed) the good news by loving and powerful deeds. That the twelve were with Him indicates that He was teaching them personally and directly through day-to-day demonstrations how they too could show or reveal the good news of the gospel. He developed such a reputation for seeking sinful men, bringing them to God and righteousness, that "the Pharisees and scribes murmured, saying, This man receiveth sinners, and eateth with them."[24] He has that reputation today, for He is still seeking to save that which was lost.

At the very beginning of Christ's ministry, the Lord told Peter and Andrew his brother, "Follow me, and I will make you fishers of men."[25] This applied to all the other disciples as well. For three years they observed Christ in His methods and followed Him in city after city, step after step, in His great mission of seeking to save that which was lost. These disciples had learned by first-hand observation and practice just how to be efficient fishers of men. Later He was to give them specific instructions where to go and what to do. At the end of His contact with Peter and the disciples, He still said to Peter, "Follow me." This same Peter tells those to whom he wrote that Christ left us an example and that we should follow in His steps.[26] Just before giving the Great Commission, the Lord sent His disciples on ahead into Galilee to a mountain which He had appointed. There they met Him and heard from Him further instructions. Go on ahead; as you have done in Galilee, so go into all the nations of the world, and I will meet you there as I have met you here. I will be with you every step of the way, even unto the end of the world. This is His personal promise to all believers. He will accompany us as we go out to the uttermost parts of the earth in His name. When He puts forth His sheep, He goes before them. We are to follow Him into the mountains and deserts of sin—from home to home, from man to man—seeking the sheep that are lost.

CHAPTER 3

INSTRUCTIONS TO SOUL WINNERS

We have seen how God Himself set the first example of visiting men in order to help them. His Son followed that example and gave His whole life seeking to save that which was lost. He went into homes to minister and win souls. He called His disciples and taught them to follow the same plan. Up and down Galilee, across Samaria, and down into Judea, the disciples learned from His example. Then the time came when He sent them on a trial expedition, giving them specific instructions about reaching the hearts of men.

THE ORIGINAL INSTRUCTIONS

In Matthew 10:1-14; Mark 6:7-13; and Luke 9:1-6, we have Jesus' detailed instructions concerning the disciples' tour into neighboring villages. Again, as recorded in Luke 10:1-6, He appointed other seventy also and sent them out. This seems to imply that Christ appointed both ministers and laymen to the task of soul winning.

TEMPORARY FEATURES

The detailed instructions found in these four passages contain a few features which had to do only with those immediate disciples and that special tour. For instance, for that particular journey He told them not to take along any money for provisions. They were to wear sandals rather than shoes and were not to take two coats. Evidently He expected them to stay overnight in certain homes and told them not to go from one house to another but to abide in the home where they were first received. He told them not to take bread with them but to eat what their hosts set before them. A distinctively temporary feature of this particular visit was that they should not go in the way of the Gentiles but only to the lost sheep of the house of Israel.

In Luke 22:35, just before His crucifixion and the beginning of the gospel dispensation, Jesus asked them, "When I sent you without purse, and scrip, and shoes, lacked ye anything? And they said, Nothing.... But now, he that hath a purse, let him take it, and likewise his scrip." This shows that instructions to personal workers were then to change. Certain features were not to be included in this new plan. From then on they could take money and clothes. Their field of operation from then on was extended beyond the Jewish boundary line. Jesus commanded in Mark 16:15, "Go ye into all the world, and preach the gospel to every creature." The gospel was to go to all Gentiles and all the world. It seems obvious, then, that time and circumstances do bring about some differences in the approach that is needed to win the lost to Christ.

CONTINUING FEATURES

There were, however, certain features in Christ's instructions to the disciples that remained the same. These continuing instructions contain valuable guidelines for us.

1. *He sent them two by two.* Mark 6:7 and Luke 10:1 both specifically note that Christ sent His dis-

ciples in pairs. This two-by-two pattern was continued
by the Early Church. In Acts 8:14, the apostles at
Jerusalem sent down to Samaria two of their number,
Peter and John, who gave the Samaritans the message
concerning the Holy Spirit. In the church at Antioch
as the disciples ministered to the Lord and fasted,
the Holy Ghost said, "Separate me Barnabas and Saul
for the work whereunto I have called them."[1] Later
Paul and Silas went together.[2] Thus the principle
of sending out disciples in pairs was confirmed and
perpetuated.

2. *He sent them to preach.* The primary purpose of
their mission under Christ's immediate personal su-
pervision remains identical with the mission of disciples today. That purpose was and is to preach the
gospel. "Go ye into all the world, and preach the
gospel to every creature."[3] "Repentance and remission of sins should be preached in his name among
all nations."[4] Not only to the lost sheep of the house
of Israel but to every creature and all nations.

3. *He equipped them with power.* Disciples are to
be equipped with power now as then. "And when he
had called unto him his twelve disciples, He gave them
power against unclean spirits, to cast them out, and
to heal all manner of sickness and all manner of disease."[5] Mark also records this provision of power which
the Lord gave His disciples then.[6] Let no one think
that Jesus has provided less supernatural assistance for
His disciples today. "These signs shall follow them
that believe; In my name shall they cast out devils;
they shall speak with new tongues; they shall take
up serpents; and if they drink any deadly thing, it
shall not hurt them; they shall lay hands on the sick,
and they shall recover."[7]

4. *He accompanies by His Spirit.* There is a feature in the present-day provision which was not possible then. He sent His disciples "before his face into every city and place, whither he himself would come."[8] He would follow them. Because of the limitation of His human body, He could not be with each group who went ahead by themselves. But now, through His Spirit, He can be with each individual who goes forth in His name to do His bidding. "Lo, I am with you alway, even unto the end of the world."[9]

5. *He warned them of rejection.* Christ prepared His disciples for a possible rejection by the people to whom they were sent. "Whosoever shall not receive you, nor hear your words, when ye depart out of that house or city, shake off the dust of your feet."[10] When Paul and Barnabas, the first pair sent forth by the Holy Ghost, were rejected by the Jews of Antioch in Pisidia, they "waxed bold, and said, It was necessary that the word of God should first have been spoken to you: but seeing you put it from you, and judge yourselves unworthy of everlasting life, lo, we turn to the Gentiles."[11] They shook off the dust of their feet against them. At Ephesus also, Paul departed from those that were hardened and believed not.[12] It appears, therefore, that the leading of the Holy Spirit, in the New Testament gospel ministry, causes the Lord's workers to turn from those who reject to others who have not heard.

6. *He required them to return and report.* Finally, after the disciples of the Lord had gone forth to preach and perform works of power in His name under His direct instruction, they returned to Him with joy, saying, "Lord, even the devils are subject unto us through thy name."[13] Paul and Barnabas also, at the

end of their first missionary journey, returned to the
church from which they had been sent, gathered the
church together, and rehearsed all that God had done
for them and how He had opened the door of faith
unto the Gentiles.[14] At the end of a subsequent missionary journey also, Paul and his company went up
to Jerusalem and the brethren received him gladly.
"And when he had saluted them, he declared particularly what things God had wrought among the
Gentiles by his ministry."[15]

THE PERMANENT INSTRUCTIONS

Many of the continuing features of Jesus' instructions to his disciples apply to us, but it is the Great
Commssion which constitutes the permanent instructions Christ gave to the disciples of this age. The
Great Commission is found in various forms in Matthew 28:19, 20; Mark 16:15-18; Luke 24:46-49; John
20:21; and Acts 1:8. The outstanding verbs of these
passages are: *go, witness, teach,* and *preach.*

GO

The disciples were told to go preach, go tell, and
go teach. The angels told the disciples "go" and
"tell."[16] Jesus said to Mary, "Go to my brethren, and
say unto them...."[17] In the Lord's parable of the
Great Supper, He said unto the servant, "Go out into
the highways and hedges."[18] To Philip, the angel of
the Lord said, "Arise and go."[19] The Lord said to
the disciple Ananias at Damascus, "Arise, and go."[20]
And there is the promise of Psalm 126:6: "He that
goeth forth and weepeth, bearing precious seed, shall
doubtless come again with rejoicing, bringing his
sheaves with him." The gospel is not written "gospel" accidentally. The very nature of the "good news"

is a command to go and spell it out to the people of the world. Maintaining the status quo is contrary to the spirit of the gospel. It is imperative that all God's disciples constantly reach out farther and farther with the gospel message, even unto the uttermost part of the earth.

WITNESS

The events to which we witness are identified in Luke 24:46-49. They are the crucifixion and resurrection of the Lord. The entire plan of salvation rests on the truth of Christ's atoning death and live-giving victory over the grave. Christ's final comments to His disciples prior to the Ascension included the prophetic command of Acts 1:8, "Ye shall receive power, after that the Holy Ghost is come upon you: and ye shall be witnesses unto me both in Jerusalem, and in all Judea, and in Samaria, and unto the uttermost part of the earth."

TEACH

The next keyword in the great commission is *teach*. Matthew's record of Jesus' parting instructions to His disciples reads: "Jesus came and spake unto them, saying, All power is given unto me in heaven and in earth. Go ye therefore, and teach all nations, baptizing them in the name of the Father, and of the Son, and of the Holy Ghost: teaching them to observe all things whosoever I have commanded you: and, lo, I am with you alway, even unto the end of the world."[21]

The instruction to teach is here mentioned twice. But it seems important that the two references do not come from the same original Greek word. In fact, they are not even synonyms. The first reference, verse 19, stems from the word meaning "make disciples of."

The second reference to teaching, verse 20, refers to the normal learning process. So our "teaching" is to carry a twofold purpose: winning, then guiding; reaching, then teaching.

A Bible description of teaching and learning appears in Isaiah 28:10, 13: "Precept upon precept, precept upon precept; line upon line, line upon line; here a little, and there a little." This requires patient, repetitious presentation of bit after bit of gospel truth until it penetrates the minds and hearts of the hearers and effects a transformation. This is what our Lord meant when He said, "Go, and teach." Teaching like this cannot be carried out in a single visit to an unconverted neighbor. In such a visit we present the first precept; it is part of the "reaching." This will be followed by the ministry of the local church in all its teaching agencies. We are commanded to reach and teach, to present the message of the gospel to the unsaved and to the growing believer who is being conformed to the image of Christ.

PREACH

Possibly the greatest keyword in the Great Commission is *preach*. "Go ye into all the world, and preach."[22] "Repentance and remission of sins should be preached."[23] "It pleased God by the foolishness of preaching to save them that believe."[24] "God . . . manifested his word through preaching."[25] These verses show us the prominence and importance of preaching in the gospel program. We need, therefore, to examine closely the accurate meaning of this word.

Here we turn to the Greek New Testament to find the various words which were translated "preach" in English. These words have shades of meaning in the

original which will be interesting and instructive.
Take the word "dianggello," which means to tell or
announce thoroughly.[26] This implies a careful, minute
preaching of the gospel. Then there is the word "dia-
legomai," to speak throughout.[27] This indicates the
widespread area in which the preaching is to be done.
"Euanggelidzo" means to tell good news or glad tidings.[28] It emphasizes the gladness of the story and the
fact that it will be good news to those who hear.
"Katanggello" means to tell thoroughly.[29] "Kerusso"
means to cry or proclaim as a herald.[30] "Laleo" is
to talk or discourse.[31] This is the conversational presentation of the gospel. Preaching is not limited to
pulpit or platform performance. In a house in Capernaum Jesus preached (laleo) unto them.[32] This is
a type of preaching which everyone can perform and
all are commanded to do so.

How the Disciples Observed the Instructions

The challenge of Christ's command to witness became the guiding force in the lives of the disciples.
Witnessing became their major task. The fact that the
Church of Jesus Christ reaches around the globe testi-
fies that those disciples did their work well.

THEY PREACHED FIRST IN JERUSALEM

Acts 1:8 can be taken as a geographical plan of
action by which the Great Commission was to be carried out: Jerusalem, Judea, Samaria, and the uttermost part of the earth. The disciples went first into
the temple at the hour of prayer. Every day in the
temple they taught and preached about Jesus Christ.
This beginning in Jerusalem fulfilled the prophecy
Jesus had related to them in Luke 24:47. The dis-

ciples did a thorough job of filling their hometown
with the gospel message.

Soon the disciples were arraigned before the high
priest to explain why they were preaching the gospel.
On one occasion the high priest railed at them and
said: "Did not we straitly command you that ye should
not teach in this name? and, behold, ye have filled
Jerusalem with your doctrine."[33] How delightful to
see that the Lord caused even His enemies to bear
witness to the extent and success of gospel's penetra-
tion into His beloved city! The disciples had indeed
begun at Jerusalem and "daily in the temple, and in
every house, they ceased not to teach and preach Jesus
Christ."[34] Because of the thorough and intensive propagation of the gospel, they influenced the whole city.
The high priest himself had to admit it. Jesus had
gone throughout every city and village. The disciples
had seen Him and learned by His example. And ac-
cordingly the disciples went throughout the city of
Jerusalem.

THEY PREACHED IN JUDEA AND SAMARIA

In predicting the spread of the gospel in Acts 1:8,
Jesus stated that His followers were to go through all
Judea. The detail of their missionary journeys in Judea
is not given in the divine record. Acts 8:1 says, "They
were all scattered abroad throughout the regions of
Judea and Samaria, except the apostles." This tells
us only that they went throughout Judea and Samaria.
In the next chapter we find the results of their witness. There were churches throughout all Judea and
Galilee and Samaria. In Acts 8:4-24 we have the story
of the great revival in the city of Samaria with the
evangelist Philip.

It must be pointed out that carrying the gospel throughout Judea and Galilee and Samaria was done under the great persecution that arose about Stephen. Thus the Lord used Satan to scatter abroad the disciples of Jerusalem. The Lord was that much in earnest about their obeying the great commandment. This reminds us of the stern measures the Lord took to scatter abroad the inhabitants of the earth when they tried to build the tower of Babel. The same pressure took the disciples as far as Phenice, Cyprus, and Antioch.

THEY PREACHED TO THE GENTILES

Two apostles were used especially to take the gospel to the Gentiles—Peter and Paul.

1. *Peter's experience at the house of Cornelius.* When Peter took the gospel to the Gentiles at Cornelius' household he reached a great juncture in gospel propagation. This was, however, preceded by the individual conversion of a Gentile as Philip led the Ethiopian eunuch to Christ.[35] A large group of Gentiles were gathered at Cornelius' house. Six Jewish brethren came with Peter and were witnesses to his preaching to the Gentiles and their acceptance of the gospel of Christ. This complete acceptance included a Pentecostal visitation of the Holy Spirit. Peter also commanded them to be baptized in the name of the Lord. When Peter went up to Jerusalem a short time later, he defended his action, and the six Jewish brethren were again witnesses. The church at Jerusalem accepted the report and glorified God, saying, "Then hath God also to the Gentiles granted repentance unto life."[36]

In the case of Peter preaching the gospel to the

Gentiles, (thus obeying the Lord's command to preach
the gospel to every creature and to teach all nations),
it must be noted that it required special urging and
guidance to help Peter understand that he should go
to Gentiles. An angel of the Lord appeared to Cornelius. As he responded, sending men to Joppa to
call for Simon Peter, the Lord gave Peter a vision at
the very time when those three men arrived at the
gate. This supernatural vision explained to him that
it was the will of God that he not call any man common or unclean. The Holy Spirit also spoke to Peter
following this vision and in coincidence of the arrival
of Cornelius' messengers, telling him to go with those
messengers, "doubting nothing: for I have sent
them."[37]

These examples of supernatural intervention succeeded in convincing Peter that he should respond to
the invitation of Cornelius and preach the gospel to
his household. God confirmed His leading by causing
the Holy Spirit to fall on Cornelius' household. It was
authenticated to Peter when he heard them "speak
with tongues and magnify God."[38] This further convinced Peter, so he exclaimed: "What was I that I
could withstand God?" Evidently this also convinced
the Jews at Jerusalem that this was the move of God.
Thus the gate was flung wide open for the preaching
of the full gospel to the Gentiles, and the Church
was on its way to a great new era, proclaiming its
testimony to all men.

2. *Paul's missionary journeys.* The Church traveled
far in spreading the gospel message, preaching first to
the Jews only and then also to the Greeks. When
they made converts at Antioch, the Church at Jerusalem was glad to hear these tidings and sent Barnabas

to assist them in growing in their Christian experience. A strong church was established at Antioch, and in turn, this church began to spread the gospel still further.

"As they ministered to the Lord, and fasted, the Holy Ghost said, Separate me Barnabas and Saul for the work whereunto I have called them. And when they had fasted and prayed, and laid their hands on tnem, they sent them away, So they, being sent forth by the Holy Ghost, departed unto Seleucia; and from thence they sailed to Cyprus."[39] They went through this island to Paphos and sailed again to Perga in Pamphilia, and Antioch in Pisidia.[40] They went on and on, through Iconium, Lystra, and Derbe, returning after completing their first missionary journey.[41]

Paul later reported, "From Jerusalem, and round about unto Illyricum (a remote province of Greece), I have fully preached the gospel of Christ."[42] He was under the compulsion of Ephesians 3:9 "to make all men see what is the fellowship of this mystery." He summarized his own ministry in Colossians 1:28, 29: "We preach, warning every man, and teaching every man in all wisdom; that we may present every man perfect in Christ Jesus: whereunto I also labour, striving according to his working, which worketh in me mightily." To the Corinthian Church he wrote, "I labored more abundantly than they all: yet not I, but the grace of God which was with me."[43] In the words of his enemies, he "turned the world upside down." The Lord was with him, and he pressed on and taught publicly and from house to house, testifying both to the Jew and also to the Greeks.

Paul left it on record that the Lord had ordained that he should be "a pattern to them which should

hereafter believe."[44] He said to the Corinthians, "Be
ye followers of me, even as I also am of Christ."[45]
And, "Wherefore I beseech you, be ye followers of
me."[46] To the Philippians he said, "Brethren, be followers together of me" and "those things which ye
have both learned, and received, and heard, and seen
in me, do."[47] Specifically, Paul taught his converts
to follow his example in spreading the gospel. Of the
Thessalonian believers he said, "From you sounded
out the word of the Lord not only in Macedonia
(their Jerusalem) and Achaia (their Judea), but also
in every place (their "uttermost part of the earth")
your faith to God-ward is spread abroad."[48] This great
apostle in his persistent pattern of house-to-house visitation and public preaching went farther and farther
out into the harvest field. He followed the instructions of Jesus. He was our example. Surely we too
are under the divine command to follow Paul as he
followed Christ.

THE RESULT—A "WITNESS" IN ALL THE WORLD

This ministry went so far in every direction that
Paul reported in Colossians 1:6 that the gospel "is
come unto you, as it is in all the world." He declared
that the gospel "was preached to every creature which
is under heaven."[49] To the Romans he said, "Yes
verily, their sound went into all the earth, and their
words unto the ends of the world."[50]

John T. Sisemore, in *The Ministry of Visitation,*
states that in less than 100 years there were as many
as 500,000 Christians.[51] Erle Cairns, in *Christianity
Through the Centuries,* estimates the size of the Church
by A.D. 250 as varying between 5 percent and 12
percent of the population of the Roman Empire.[52]

Thus the first generation of Christians discharged their responsibility to their contemporaries throughout the whole world, even as the Lord had commanded them. That generation did not have modern conveniences nor the latest methods of travel and communication. But they had all that was necessary. They had the command of the Lord Jesus Christ, His personal presence with them and the power of the Holy Spirit with which to preach the gospel and to perform wonders in His name.

CHAPTER 4

PREPARATION FOR SOUL WINNING

After considering the magnificent accomplishment of the first generation of disciples, let us now look at the task which lies before us today. Jesus said, "Say not ye, There are yet four months, and then cometh harvest? behold, I say unto you, Lift up your eyes, and look on the fields; for they are white already to harvest."[1]

A Look at the Field

In obedience to this command, we lift up our eyes even to the remote horizons and look carefully and long at the fields which await our reaping. As we observed the path of the early disciples in fulfilling Acts 1:8, let us consider what a similar path would mean to us. "Ye shall be witnesses unto me— (1) both in Jerusalem, (2) and in all Judea, (3) and in Samaria and (4) unto the uttermost part of the earth."

BEGINNING AT JERUSALEM

Jesus told His disciples in Luke 24:47 that they should begin their gospel preaching in Jerusalem. For us the term *Jerusalem* can have several meanings. Good interpretation requires that first of all we take the literal, natural explanation.

1. *The actual city.* At the moment Jerusalem is in a pitiful condition. Situated on the border between Jordan and Israel, it is cut in half by the line dividing these opposing states. A narrow no-man's-land with a barbed wire fence separates the two halves of the city. Many years ago the Master looked upon His beloved city and said, "O Jerusalem, Jerusalem, thou that killest the prophets, and stonest them which are sent unto thee, how often would I have gathered thy children together, even as a hen gathereth her chickens under her wings, and ye would not!"[2] Surely, such love has not diminished; He still longs for the salvation of His beloved city.

The missionaries of the first century were specifically told to go first of all to the Jews. In describing the gospel of Christ, Paul said, "It is the power of God unto salvation to every one that believeth; to the Jew first, and also to the Greek."[3] This must indeed still be the order. The Lord loves the Jews of this generation just as He loved the Jews of Paul's time. There are now more Jews in New York City than in all of Palestine. Over 5,000,000 Jews live in the United States, and the world Jewish population is about 13,000,000. They are that part of the great worldwide harvest field to which our Lord tells us to give priority in our gospel ministry.

2. *Our Jerusalem.* There is also a sense in which the term *Jerusalem* refers to our own hometown or city. The Jewish disciples, by beginning at Jerusalem, began at their home base. Their immediate neighbors and friends were the ones to whom they first began to witness. They pushed out the circle of their activity until it filled the whole city. No wonder they succeeded so well; for "daily in the temple, and in

every house, they ceased not to teach and preach Jesus Christ."[4]

We too must witness in our own hometowns. We must stand on our own street corners. We must ring our own neighbor's doorbells. In every house we should not cease to teach and preach, even daily, the wonderful news of salvation. No one is qualified or worthy to carry the gospel beyond the borders of his hometown and native country until he first perseveres in witnessing at home. Our own personal "Jerusalem" is indicated by Christ as our first objective in gospel propagation.

We should not overlook the word "both" which precedes the detail of the various points of ministry cited in this verse. It seems that the Master was emphasizing that no one place should be occupied at the expense of the other. Both should be occupied simultaneously.

ON TO JUDEA

The United States of America can be considered our "Judea." According to the *World Almanac,* the population of the United States is about 190,000,000. In this country there are about 116,000,000 church members, according to the *Yearbook of American Churches.* The following is an approximate general division of the religious communities included in the above number of church members:

Protestants (all groups) 61,000,000
Catholics (all groups) 46,000,000
Jews 5,000,000
Cults 4,000,000

From the above we see that there are over 74,000,000 people who are not listed as even being religious, for their names are not on the roll of any church or religious society in the United States. The unchurched usually admit that they are not saved. Most of the cultists do not believe in Jesus Christ whose blood saves sinners; therefore, we cannot accept them as saved people. It may be that some members of the various Catholic churches of the United States know the Lord as their Saviour. On the other hand, most of them apparently hope for salvation by works. Also, their dependence on their church, their priests, and the Virgin Mary rather than upon our Lord Jesus and His substitutionary death alone, raises grave doubt as to their salvation.

What about the various Protestant church members? Many churches substitute ritual for real salvation, and many church members have only nominal faith. Can we believe they are really born-again Christians? Many of them are outside the fold of the redeemed and constitute a part of the great harvest field into which the Lord has sent us to reap.

This examination indicates that over one half of the citizens of the United States are probably lost and without God. We are face to face with a great harvest field of about 100 million people right here at home who are not saved. They are dear to the heart of the Shepherd, and He wants His undershepherds to go after those that are lost.

ON TO SAMARIA

The next category of people that make up the world harvest field are those that can be designated as "Samaria." The province of Samaria lay in the immediate pathway of the expanding church. It was the city of Samaria, in the province of Samaria to which

Philip went as described in Acts 8:5-25. The Samaritans
of those days were half Jew and half Gentile. Generations earlier, an Assyrian king had transported most
of the ten tribes of Israel into captivity. He replaced
them in the cities of Samaria with people sent back
from Babylon and other cities. These imported hea-
then mingled with the original inhabitants of the land
and produced the mixed race known as Samaritans.
They had their own place and method of worship.
The Jews had no dealings with the Samaritans. In
spite of this, the Lord Jesus made the Good Samaritan
the hero of one of His most well-known parables.
He also called attention to the fact that the one leper
who returned to give him thanks was "a stranger,"
a Samaritan.[5] His lengthy conversation with the woman
at the well also proves His utter disregard of social
distinctions.

We, too, have a Samaria into which we must carry
the gospel. There are people in our society who are
socially estranged. The great integration struggle in
which we are now engaged is striking contemporary
evidence of this fact. Also a shadow of anti-Semitism
lies over our country. Distinctions sometimes arise between American Indians and other present-day Ameri-
cans although time is easing this tension. Sometimes
the foreign-born among us feel estranged. How beautiful that the Lord designated all these people as worthy
of our attention and evangelization. We must not ignore
them. They must not be neglected in the onward
march of the Church as it carries the story of redemption to every kindred, tribe, and tongue.

ON TO THE UTTERMOST PART

From this point our vision reaches out unto the

great worldwide harvest which Jesus called the "uttermost part of the earth." From Samaria the disciples were scattered abroad. They went to Cyprus and to Antioch and then throughout Asia Minor and across into Macedonia. From there to Rome and Spain. History picks up the story and tells us that they went all over North Africa, as far east as India and as far north as England. In that generation, disciples reached the uttermost part of the earth they knew. Since then a new hemisphere has been discovered. North and South America, China, Japan, and other areas of Asia, Africa south of the Sahara, and the islands of the sea fill out the present-day world harvest field.

There are approximately three billion people in the world. From the standpoint of ideology, it can be said that Communism holds sway over one-third of these people. Another third are in the "Christian world" (meaning they are Protestants or Catholics). The rest of the world comprises the remaining third.

Only God knows the people in His big, wide world who are truly right with Him and whose souls are ready for eternity. All the rest are without God and without hope. Yet, our Lord tried to save them *all*. They were made in the image of God and, as such, are potential sons and daughters of God. He is not willing that any should perish. He would have all men to be saved. God has sent His children into all the world to preach the gospel to every creature. Will we not hearken to this call and be His messengers to bring the wondrous glad tidings of His love and their possible redemption?

A Look at Ourselves

As we contemplate service in the harvest field, let

us see what spiritual preparation we will need.

REGENERATION, THE FIRST REQUISITE

First, a worker must have a genuine born-again experience. True visitation evangelism can never be performed by one who is trying to "work his way to heaven."

BAPTISM IN THE SPIRIT, THE SECOND REQUISITE

When the Lord laid on His disciples the great obligation of telling the story of His redeeming grace, He commanded them to wait in Jerusalem until they had been baptized in the Holy Spirit.[6] Jesus Himself had received this infilling.[7] The early disciples received the experience.[8] Can any modern-day disciples consider it unnecessary to be baptized in the Holy Spirit?

It is the will of God that all believers be empowered for service. We need the power of the Holy Spirit to preach the gospel, to win souls to Christ, to heal the sick, to endure persecution, to withstand opposition, and to press forward to the "uttermost part of the earth." We may have that power, for "the promise is unto you, and to your children, and to all that are afar off, even as many as the Lord our God shall call."[9] The baptism in the Holy Spirit is essential preparation for carrying out the Great Commission.

1. *The worker must use the power of the Spirit.* Many people today have received the baptism in the Holy Spirit. What responsibility they have to use that power given them through the Spirit! Army uniforms and weapons of war are not primarily for dress parade. Jesus gave His disciples power to cast out devils and heal the sick; they *used* this power when He sent them on their first gospel journey. On their return, they

rejoiced that the devils were subject unto them.[10] The same thing happened later when they were sent on the permanent assignment.[11] What about this generation of disciples? We are instructed and empowered to carry the gospel. Do we go and return with the thrilling testimony of victory?

2. *The worker must remain filled with the Spirit.* To have received the baptism in the Spirit and to remain "filled with the Spirit" are two different things. Peter was "filled with the Holy Ghost" when he spoke to the Sanhedrin some time after he was originally filled with the Spirit.[12] The same was true of Stephen and Paul.[13] "Be filled with the Spirit"—"Continue being filled" is the injunction. "If we live in the Spirit let us also walk in the Spirit," producing the fruit of the Spirit. The Spirit of Christ is the Spirit of evangelism, and this Spirit must find expression in order to survive.

3. *The worker must seek the guidance of the Spirit.* Being filled with the Spirit provides the personal guidance and leadership of the Holy Spirit. "For as many as are led by the Spirit of God, they are the sons of God."[14] When Christ instructed His disciples, He said, "Take no thought how or what ye shall speak: for it shall be given you in that same hour what ye shall speak. For it is not ye that speak, but the Spirit of your Father which speaketh in you."[15] Since the Holy Spirit will supply words and testimony in the hour of personal peril, we can surely count on Him to supply the words needed in visitation work. So, count on the Holy Spirit to guide and help you, and you will not trust in vain.

4. *The worker must have a love for souls and faith.* Out of the Spirit-filled Christian life, there flows a

love for souls. Love will prompt us to seek their personal salvation. Love will give us patience and kindness to deal with anyone who needs the gospel.

This same Spirit-filled life produces the faith needed for success. Peter said of a man who had been healed, "The faith which is by him hath given him this perfect soundness in the presence of you all."[16] Paul said, "The life which I now live in the flesh I live by the faith of the Son of God, who loved me, and gave himself for me."[17] This is the secret of a faith that triumphs. We shall need faith to trust in the Spirit's leading, to procure the needed wisdom. Our Lord said that He would make us fishers of men, so we can believe He will do just that.

5. *The worker must seek a replenishing of the Spirit.* Strange as it may seem, the Christian must continuously replenish his supply of power, love, and faith. Paul wrote, "Not that we are sufficient of ourselves . . . but our sufficiency is of God."[18] Is this not the message of Isaiah 40:31, "They that wait upon the Lord shall renew their strength"? It is why Paul exhorted us to pray without ceasing and to continue instant in prayer.[19]

CHRISTIAN CHARACTER, THE THIRD REQUISITE

A soul winner needs to guard his reputation and exhibit at all times a character that is truly Christian. He should live free from unwholesome habits and have a conversation that is known by its godliness. The soul winner represents the Christian life; he should not be guilty of worldliness or sin. It is futile for a person to speak of righteousness when his private life is known to be lacking that very quality. A Christian witness whose life agrees with his description of God's grace is one of the best testimonies a person can have.

PRAYER, A FUNDAMENTAL NECESSITY

Prayer is fundamental to success in house-to-house visitation. It prefaced all the activities of the early disciples. Peter and John went to the temple at the hour of prayer.[20] After their first trial before the Sanhedrin, they joined their fellow disciples and lifted up their voices to God in prayer.[21] The apostles gave themselves continually to prayer and to the ministry of the Word.[22] It was when the disciples at Antioch fasted and prayed that the Holy Ghost sent forth Barnabas and Saul to missionary activity.[23] Prayer undergirds all Christian endeavor. It is vital to effective soul winning.

COMPASSION, AN INDISPENSABLE QUALITY

A Spirit-filled life of constant prayer will produce a tender compassion for the lost. When Jesus came over the brow of the hill at Bethany on His triumphant ride toward Jerusalem on that first Palm Sunday, He broke into tears as He looked upon His beloved city. He did not fear the suffering that awaited Him there, but He lamented that Jerusalem was unaware that she would shortly be overwhelmed by her enemies.[24] Our hearts too should be moved with compassion as was His when He looked upon the multitudes who were as sheep without a shepherd.[25]

The Apostle Paul had this same tenderhearted ministry. In Acts 20:19 he tells about his ministry to the church at Ephesus, where he "served the Lord with all humility of mind, and with many tears." In one of his letters to the church at Corinth, he said, "Out of much affliction and anguish of heart I wrote unto you with many tears."[26]

Compassion was characteristic of sincere servants of God in all ages past. David said, "My tears have been my meat day and night."[27] Joel called for the ministers of the Lord to gird themselves and lament and weep between the porch and the altar.[28] Ezekiel saw the seal of safety put on those who "that sigh and that cry for all the abominations that be done" in Jerusalem.[29] Jeremiah was a weeping prophet.[30] Daniel mourned three full weeks.[31] Nehemiah too wept and mourned when he heard of the humiliation of Jerusalem.[32] This was the expression of love shown by God's men of old.

It is a principle of the Word: "They that sow in tears shall reap in joy. He that goeth forth and weepeth, bearing precious seed, shall doubtless come again with rejoicing, bringing his sheaves with him."[33] First, there is a going forth. This is in perfect harmony with the first command of the Great Commission, "Go." But our "going" must be governed by our compassion for those to whom we go.

Jesus and Paul are examples of those whose hearts were moved to tears when dealing with men. The precious seed is to be watered with tears. That seed is not a story about the local church nor even about the fine pastor. The seed is the word of God, and this will spring up and bear fruit to the glory of God. Then comes the glad assurance and the fulfillment of promise: We shall doubtless come again with rejoicing, bringing our sheaves with us. Our joy will be full when we can lay those sheaves at His feet.

PRACTICAL VIRTUES, THE OUTGROWTH OF CHRISTIAN LIVING

True spiritual warmth and reality always find expression in practical virtues and characteristics. Such qualifications reveal their true value and usefulness in visitation work.

1. *Courage.* It takes courage to ring a doorbell and stand face to face with a stranger. The disciple Ananias shrank from the Lord's assignment to him of visiting Saul of Tarsus who had just arrived in Damascus. Saul's reputation was fearsome, and Ananias reminded the Lord that this man had come to arrest him and the other Christians who lived there. But the Lord insisted that he go, and Ananias took courage and went. It was his great delight to find that Saul had met Jesus on the way, was already converted, and was expecting Ananias to come and help him in his new-found spiritual experience. Who knows but that you too will be thrilled to find hungry hearts, just waiting for someone to tell them how to find the Lord. "Be strong and of a good courage; be not afraid, neither be thou dismayed: for the Lord thy God is with thee withersoever thou goest."[34]

2. *Friendliness.* One's attitude in approaching a person is very important. There should be a smile and an easy unaffected friendliness on the part of the visitor. To make friends, you must be friendly yourself.[35] A cordial, unassuming friendliness will be a stimulant to conversation and contribute greatly to the success of your work. Be kind, warm, and courteous. It has been said that you will never catch a fish by throwing stones at him.

3. *Tact.* Not everyone has the gift of tact, and those who do not, find misfortune aplenty! Tact will help us use great wisdom and care in all we say, remembering never to criticize or in any way to offend those whom we wish to win for the Lord. No derogatory

comment should be made at any time, and whenever possible, complimentary words should be spoken. In essence, tact is good manners.

4. *Sympathy.* It could be possible that a situation will come to light which calls for an expression of sympathy from the visitor. This will present an opportunity to show the love of Christ, which in turn will open hearts. In a time of need, nothing is more appreciated than an expression of love and kindness. Let your sincere and genuine sympathy be given unhesitatingly.

5. *Patience.* It is human nature to resist or evade an approach of the Holy Spirit. So the worker can expect to encounter some reluctance as he seeks to lead a soul to Christ. Interruptions and diversions will call for patience on the part of the worker. At these times conversation should be tactfully returned to the point, which is the prospect's spiritual welfare. Never become impatient or irritated. Quietly and kindly endeavor to press the point to a successful conclusion.

6. *Persistence.* Patience often develops into persistence, which is a quality the visitor should seek to manifest. There is a point, however, where persistence can become offensive, and at this point it should be modified. When resentment is noticed, it is time to cease pressing the point. More damage than good might otherwise be done. At this point trust the Lord to give guidance.

7. *Ethics.* A word should be said about ethics. Conversation could possibly become so friendly as to include personal confidences. In such a situation, let us be sure to take a "professional" attitude. In other words, remember that it is strictly unethical ever, at any time, to betray a confidence given in sacred trust.

There is a world to win, and it lies waiting before us. But we must remember that it begins right at our doorstep. If we are ready—fully prepared—the Lord is ready to use us in winning the lost to Him.

CHAPTER 5

WAYS OF WINNING SOULS

The examples brought to us through the life of Christ and the early disciples show us that men and women can be led to faith in many places and in many ways. A crowded seashore, a lonely well, a night-time interview, a busy street—the message went to the people wherever they were found.

Modern science has increased the number of ways we can spread the gospel, and the Holy Spirit is ready to use this variety. But in the midst of this variety, we recall once more that over and over Christ and the apostles found personal encounters one of the most effective way to witness. Christians must know and use every available means of reaching the lost. Only by doing so will we fulfill the commands of Christ.

In this chapter we will consider the various ways a person may witness, the ways he can locate prospects to whom he will witness, and the ways prospects may be visited.

WAYS OF WITNESSING

Every means of communication available today has been used to proclaim the message of the gospel. Each medium has both advantages and limitations. A knowledge of these witnessing opportunities will help the Church increase its evangelistic outreach.

MASS EVANGELISM

The New Testament tells of great crowds that followed Jesus. They came to hear Him preach and to benefit from His healing ministry. From that time until now, vast crowds have congregated to hear the gospel of salvation preached. Curiosity, concern, interest, and need have all been responsible for bringing people to hear the preacher.

1. *Special campaigns.* Mass evangelism is still a vital part of spreading the gospel. City-wide campaigns, tent, stadium, and cooperative meetings all provide opportunities for witnessing to the claims of Christ.

2. *Regular church services.* Continuing opportunities to exalt Christ as Saviour and Redeemer are offered in the regular services of the church. The emphasis given to evangelism will determine how effective the local church is in winning men to Christ. Dr. Charles Price once stated, "You will secure results in whatever you emphasize the most." When the pastor, his deacons, and other departmental officers are committed to win souls, there will be a continual ingathering of men and women to Christ.

3. *Radio services.* Radio offers both the local and the national church unusual opportunities to introduce Christ to the unsaved. More radio receivers are in use than ever before. In cars, boats, on picnics, and at the beach, people have radios with them. Persons though completely shut off from any gospel witness may be reached by radio.

4. *Television services.* Nearly half the populace of the United States views television programs regularly.

More widespread use of television by churches will develop in the future. Each church needs to study its local broadcasting opportunities to discover how it may use television locally for witnessing to the saving power of Christ.

5. *Films.* An increasing number of motion picture films are available to the church to tell the story of Christ's redeeming power. Many stories of unusual conversions have been filmed. These films make a powerful impression upon young people.

6. *Distribution of literature.* Modern printing has given the church opportunity to witness through literature. Attractive, powerful written messages may be placed in the hands of people who would not permit anyone to talk with them. Literature has a long life-span and usually results in a series of contacts for each printed item. It is good that the church is becoming more effective in its use of literature for communicating the gospel of Christ.

PERSONAL EVANGELISM

Jesus continually turned casual encounters into soul-winning opportunities. He welcomed Andrew to His home where He revealed Himself as the Messiah. Immediately Andrew went out and won Peter. Passing by Matthew at the receipt of customs, Jesus bid him to follow, and Matthew did. Jesus' informal meeting with the Centurion resulted in a witness which remains to this day a challenge to every worker.

Every Christian should be prepared through training and experience to turn casual encounters into witnessing opportunities. When trained and directed by the Holy Spirit, this method can become one of the most productive ways to win souls to the Lord.

1. *Conversational evangelism.* Private conversation often turns to religion. Believers use these opportunities to explain their faith and to invite unbelievers to their churches. It often would require little more conversation to lead an interested person to the Lord right during such a conversation. This is witnessing to people where you find them, winning the ones you can, and placing the others in a favorable position to receive follow-up visits from other Christians in your church.

2. *House-to-house evangelism.* House-to-house calling may appear a laborious mission, but it need not be. It is the apostolic pattern for witnessing. A wide-open field for personal evangelism, it is a challenge to every Christian worker. Here is high adventure for Christ. Every home presents a new kind of opportunity in witnessing. Some may look unfavorably upon your visit, but in most instances the personal worker is treated kindly even if his message is not accepted.

Thorough training in the techniques of soul winning will make personal witnessing easier. When a worker learns how to win a sinner's confidence, he has lessened the possibility of antagonism. A soul won to the Lord in this way will stimulate the worker to increase his activity in personal witnessing.

3. *Telephone evangelism.* A new phase of witnessing is developing. By using the telephone, persons in all walks of life and in remote areas of your community may be reached easily and swiftly. Called "telewitnessing," it makes possible the discovery of many persons who have spiritual needs. A follow-up visit may be arranged or the person may be invited to your church.

By following a plan, each block of the city for which

your church is responsible may be covered systematically. A cross-reference directory listing residence by streets may be used for this purpose. Age and infirmities are not necessarily handicaps to the worker. This type of personal evangelism will offer everyone who engages in it many thrilling experiences. Each new telephone call will be a spiritual challenge:

STRENGTHS AND WEAKNESSES

Every method of witnessing has valid reasons to support its continuance. A general "sowdown" of a community with soul-winning literature may be accomplished with workers of all ages and experience. With a minimum of instructions, the workers can go house-to-house and leave a literature piece with anyone in the home. When done with a cheery smile and enthusiasm, it can make a lasting impression.

This can be a way to quickly reach a whole community with a gospel witness. A corp of workers with a special piece of gospel literature can easily reach fifty homes per worker in a two-hour period. With the inclusion of an invitation to attend your church, this may be an effective way to give a witness for Christ and present your church as a good place to worship God.

All ages may participate in this literature sowdown, but it is particularly adaptable to the young people. This method may be used to introduce them into a lifetime of personal witnessing. Many of their fears may be overcome, and they will discover the joys of service to the Lord.

Since only a brief contact is made at each home, it is quite possible that many homes where there is spiritual interest will be passed by. Only the most obvious cases of need will come to light.

On the other hand, direct personal witnessing may be more successful in learning about a greater number of persons who have need of spiritual help or who have definite interest in spiritual matters. Although slower in covering an area, sometimes with the making of only one call an hour, it is possible to attempt to be of help in each home.

Training is necessary to pursue direct personal witnessing. The worker must know how to get the attention and interest of the prospect. The scriptural principles which will lead a person to accept Christ as his personal Saviour must be learned so they can be explained to the sinner. This will require time and dedication, but it will repay in rich dividends with souls saved.

WAYS TO LOCATE PROSPECTS

When the soul winner has become interested in personally witnessing to the unsaved, he wants to find people to whom he may witness. It is easy to say that he should witness to everyone he sees, but doing this with any high degree of success is unlikely.

Like drilling for oil, the soul winner needs to know where to look for those who may be prospects to whom to witness. Locating the names of people is not difficult today—the telephone directory is full of them, but to find people who are interested to some degree in spiritual matters requires a thorough understanding of the ways to identify the "qualified prospect."

THROUGH THE SUNDAY SCHOOL

Most common and most easily accessible to the church worker are the prospects secured from the Sunday school records. Alert teachers list class visitors and discover potential students who make excellent prospects for personal witnessing visits. It is a help later if teachers will get as much accurate information as possible about the prospect.

THROUGH REGULAR CHURCH SERVICES

Many persons attend the church simply out of curiosity, but they may become spiritually concerned as they return from time to time. Each church should devise its own plan to secure the names of all visitors and interested friends. These persons should provide a list of good "qualified prospects."

THROUGH SPECIAL CHURCH GROUPS

Persons may become interested in the church through the church activities, such as the Women's Missionary Council or Men's Fellowship. Persons introduced to the life of the church through these groups may not be saved. If they are not, they should be included immediately in the prospect list for a visit from one of the personal workers. When listing information about the person, it is helpful to know which group brought him in contact with the church.

THROUGH SPECIAL MEETINGS

City-wide evangelistic campaigns, cooperative meetings, and revival services all offer programs which appeal especially to the unsaved. Every name secured in one of these mass evangelism meetings should be considered a good prospect.

THROUGH FRIENDLY INQUIRERS

Every member of the church should be constantly alert to secure the names and addresses of persons who indicate interest in the church or ask for spiritual guidance. An immediate visit should be made to them by a skilled soul winner.

THROUGH NEWS ACCOUNTS OF CHURCH ACTIVITIES

Every church has many opportunities for publicity about its activities. The daily or weekly newspapers usually provide space, free of charge, each week for the church to tell its story. A well-written news item can direct the attention of many to your church. While an indirect way of witnessing, it can, nevertheless, be effective.

In many areas both radio and television stations provide public service time for brief church announcements. To fulfill its witnessing ministry to its community, every church should use these media of communication to interest the unsaved in Christ.

Often as a direct result of such publicity, people will call the church office asking for further information about the church. Some people may have acquaintances in the church and question them about the publicity. These persons will welcome callers from the church.

THROUGH PERSONAL CONTACTS

Like the salesman who finds prospects for his products among all his daily contacts, the soul winner should be sensitive and alert to the needs of those with whom he associates each day.

The church should make every member a special envoy to the area in which he lives and works. It should be his main duty to find the names and addresses of persons who are unsaved and need to be visited by a personal worker.

THROUGH PUBLIC INSTITUTIONS

Prisons, detention homes, hospitals, nursing and rest homes, sanitariums, and other public institutions offer opportunities for personal witnessing. Not only are those who hear the message through the gospel services in the institutions affected by it, but often contacts are made with unsaved members of the families. Many of these persons will appreciate a church caller visiting them. Thus a wide spectrum of prospects is opened to the observant workers.

THROUGH CHURCH MAILINGS

Churches using a mail contact with its members and friends find it another prospect source. As names are added to the mailing list, they become qualified prospects for the personal worker.

THROUGH LITERATURE DISTRIBUTION

A regular part of every church's program should be literature distribution. Saturation distribution of literature should be carried out periodically in the neighborhood of the church and throughout the city.

Attractive handout pieces such as *The Pentecostal Evangel,* tracts from the Sunday School Department and Christ's Ambassadors Department, and *Revivaltime's* summer soul-winning miniature books, will demand a high degree of readership. In turn, inquirers and visitors will come to the church and will become prospects for the church visitors.

THROUGH A SURVEY

An area or city-wide survey provides valuable information about unreached homes. These surveys should be frequent enough to keep up with the population shifts. Many people will be uncovered who have dormant spiritual interests.

THROUGH A "PROSPECT" CAMPAIGN

At least once a year each church should have a "prospect" campaign. This is a plan whereby the members of the church will turn in the names and addresses of people interested in the church or concerned about spiritual things. It should be carried over a three-week period to secure the maximum results. The degree of interest the prospect shows in the church should be carefully recorded for the use of the personal worker. This campaign can prove one of the most profitable activities of the church year if a well-planned follow-up program is carried out.

THROUGH REFERRALS

There are always people who turn to the church for assistance and guidance. Your church will get the names of such persons. Insofar as possible, it is desirable that a personal worker visit them and endeavor to render such assistance as is possible. Often in the process of helping a needy family, souls are won to the Lord.

THROUGH COFFEE KLATCHES AND BIBLE GROUPS

Most neighbors have coffee klatches. These and neighborhood Bible study groups are excellent opportunities for finding prospects for soul-winning visitation. Through the informal conversation, it will be possible to learn the spiritual needs and interests of the neighbors.

THROUGH NEWCOMER AND UTILITIES LISTS

Most communities have some kind of service to

identify and give recognition to the newcomers. It may be a "Welcome Wagon" service or a listing of new customers by the utilities company. Whichever it is, the church should make the most of it.

THROUGH "TELEWITNESSING"

Use of the telephone to locate persons with spiritual interest is proving increasingly valuable. Without leaving home a person may call upon any number of persons and learn about their spiritual needs. Where sufficient interest is shown an appointment for a personal visit may be set up.

THROUGH DOOR-TO-DOOR CALLING

In place of engaging in a census, it may be desirable to carry on a door-to-door calling campaign. Many opportunities will arise for immediate witnessing. On the other hand, there will be many names secured of persons who will either desire or need to have the personal workers from the church visit them. Cards for listing these persons should be carried at all times so complete information may be recorded.

THROUGH NEWSPAPER ADS

Increasing interest has been aroused in placing denominational ads in the newspapers explaining our doctrines. Inquiries should result from these wherever they are run. All inquiries should be followed up by the local church.

THROUGH RADIO AND TELEVISION SERVICES

If your church has a radio or television broadcast, design it so there will be audience response to it. Many who listen have serious physical and spiritual needs. Your service may encourage them to look to the Lord for help. If you solicit their response, they will write requesting prayer. A visit to them may be arranged. Some giveaway item may be offered to attract them to write. Personal workers should be prepared to visit them if it seems desirable.

THROUGH A COUNSELING SERVICE

Your church may support a counseling service, either through the church itself or in cooperation with other churches. A by-product of this service will be the names of families or individuals who need a church visitor to call upon them. The names secured through this service will be highly qualified in most instances. Follow-up should be made as soon as the names are secured.

WAYS TO VISIT

How a person approaches his visitation work is important. If he visits with the purpose of urging a visitor to return to Sunday school or church, the result will probably be just that. But if he visits with the purpose of winning a soul to Christ, the probable result will be a new convert. The purpose of a visit largely determines the results of the visit.

If you wish to win men directly to Christ when you visit them, you will need to plan each step you will take. Let us discuss the ways to visit your prospect and evaluate each.

FRIENDSHIP CALLS

In some instances the Christian workers should first cultivate friendship with the persons to whom they plan to witness. Several calls may be necessary before the friendship develops to the point where it is possible to present a successful witness for Christ. The first step in friendship is gaining the confidence of the prospect. A friendly, personal conversation which shows interest in the home, in the activities of its occupants and their needs, will go far in building confidence and friendship. When a good rapport and friendly relationships have been developed, the workers can then make an introduction of Christ and have some assurance that their witnessing will be received.

SUNDAY SCHOOL AND CHURCH INVITATION CALLS

Since many of the visitation programs are initiated through the church and Sunday school, it has sometimes been assumed that the chief purpose of any caller is to give an invitation to attend these meetings. This is not always true.

Sunday school growth, however, does require a vigorous and consistent visitation plan designed to present the advantages of attending the particular church and its Sunday school. Enthusiasm for the church and its program produces an effective invitation. It must be understood that the ultimate reason for inviting persons to church and Sunday school is to instruct them in the Bible so they may accept Jesus Christ as their Saviour. However, this may not be stressed or even mentioned in this kind of visiting.

BIBLE TEACHING CALLS

Many persons reside in each community who, because of circumstances of life, have had little contact with the church and consequently know little about the gospel of Jesus Christ. Before they can be led to accept Him as their Saviour, they must be taught some of the fundamentals of the Christian faith.

In the Early Church the disciples "ceased not to teach daily in the temple and in every house." The need to teach in every house is greater today than ever before. When people do not understand the basic principles of the Word of God, they will not commit themselves to its cause. When visiting such people, we need to teach the main truths of the gospel that lay a foundation for faith in Christ.

CENSUS CALLS

A census will give you a clear picture of the people in your community who need to be reached with the gospel. This requires extensive planning, adequate records, and thorough organization to successfully carry the census to a completion.

For the workers who will actually go house-to-house, making contact with the householders, this will provide an introduction to calling and make future personal witnessing easier.

LITERATURE CALLS

A double-pronged approach can be made to a part or the whole of a community by the house-to-house distribution of literature. This is accomplished by making a personal contact when handing out each piece of literature.

Attractive, well-prepared literature will carry a message into the home where it may remain for a long time. Many persons in the home may read it, and in some instances conversions will result.

By reaching each house and making a personal presentation of the literature, it is highly probably that the caller will find some persons concerned about spiritual matters. Either a great need in the home or an unsatisfied spiritual longing may prompt the worker to pursue his witnessing plan further. The happy combination of giving literature directly to the householder has made this method of great value.

SOUL-WINNING CALLS

A soul-winning call has as its immediate objective an organized presentation of the plan of salvation and the winning of the prospect to Christ. The first step is, of course, to obtain an opportunity for conversation. A warm, friendly attitude at the door or when meeting a person helps prepare him to receive your message. Then it will be possible to introduce into the conversation a consideration of spiritual things. A logical result of the conversation will be a presentation of the scriptural basis of salvation.

Because it has been the purpose of the caller to lead the prospect to accept Christ as his Saviour immediately, he will press for a decision. His planned approach will make this possible.

This is the most important kind of calling; it should be given the greatest attention, both in preparation and in use. Alert workers will find that any type of call may develop into a soul-winning call.

With so many social, political, and technological changes being made today, the church is no longer the center of attraction in the community. It is necessary to bridge the gap between the church and the world. Thus, it has become mandatory that Christian workers return to the apostolic pattern of witnessing. We must fill our "Jerusalem" with the witness of Jesus Christ. This witness will achieve its greatest results through a person-to-person encounter.

CHAPTER **6**

OPENING THE SOUL-WINNING CONVERSATION

...APPROACH AND TRANSITION

"There was a man of the Pharisees, named Nicodemus . . . the same came to Jesus."[1] Nicodemus made the approach and Jesus turned the conversation. Then followed the great sermon on the new birth. Happy is the soul winner who has such an experience, when the seeker comes to him and makes the approach. But how often does it occur? Can one justifiably wait for it to occur? The answer is contained in the next chapter of John's gospel. Here Christ explained that "he must needs go through Samaria."[2]

The Record states that a Samaritan woman came to draw water as Jesus paused at Jacob's well to rest. Jesus said, "Give me to drink." This time Jesus, having been led by the Spirit, made the approach and then turned the conversation to spiritual things. Again a great sermon followed dealing with living water and true spiritual worship. In the case of Nicodemus the conversion was left in doubt; in the case of the Samaritan woman, faith was expressed openly. Many believed, in turn, because of the woman's testimony. Many more of her fellow citizens believed after they had heard Jesus for themselves.

Sometimes they come to us! Usually we must "go" to them! There is no command in the Scripture to the unsaved telling him to "go to the church, to find a believer and ask him the way of salvation." But there is an abundance of injunction to the believer telling him to "go and tell!"

We might wish the sinner would always make the approach. But since this is not the usual experience, the essential evangelism is an "everywhere, everyday, every believer" kind of evangelism, a friendship evangelism that is ready to go into action at every opportunity. This is an ideal evangelism that penetrates all areas of society and constantly exposes Jesus. Also, it is in order to set aside special times to go to "target areas" even as Jesus sent out His disciples.[3]

When one purposes to engage friends in conversation for Christ or to "go on purpose," as it were, he immediately asks himself: "Just what am I to do? How can I break the grip of fear which has stopped me before? What shall I say first? How can I turn the conversation to spiritual things and toward Christ?" It is these questions that we discuss in this chapter.

THE NATURE OF THE SOUL WINNING CONFRONTATION

It will be helpful first to observe just what is to be done. Too often there is a preoccupation with method to the neglect of essential purpose. *In essence the soul-winning encounter is a confrontation of Christ in His followers, by the Holy Spirit, in love, in His name, and with an unbeliever.*

The purpose of the soul-winning confrontation is *to show* Christ in life, in deed, and in word. The soul winner is not sent to argue but to witness, not to win a debate but to win a soul, not to show his knowledge of the Word but *to show Jesus.* He is sent as a winner, as a reaper to reap the harvest where he finds it![4]

The soul winner must go working with the Spirit. When he follows this principle, he has the confidence that *he will either be led to help develop a harvest or led to a harvest that is ready to be reaped.* This makes all "going" purposeful and profitable. Seldom is a person saved immediately as a result of one encounter. Usually a conversion results from a series of encounters, experiences, and impressions. Therefore, during an encounter, when there is little or no apparent response, the worker knows the harvest is not yet ready, but he also knows that the Holy Spirit, who led him to make a contribution to the conversion of a particular sinner, will continue His work. Led by the Spirit, he will carefully do what he can to contribute to an ultimate harvest and then will graciously close the encounter for that time. He knows many may sow and water; someone will reap!

OVERCOMING THE FEAR-GUILT CYCLE

Fear and a sense of guilt are the elements of a vicious cycle which inhibits soul winners. Fear results in a failure to witness and win souls which, in turn, results in a sense of guilt. This sense of guilt contributes to a loss of spiritual victory and a weakness of spiritual life, which, in turn, incites fear. Adam's testimony was this: "I was afraid . . . and I hid myself."[5] How similar this is to the "testimony" of many Christians!

Fear is faithlessness, the absence of faith. It results from being out of proper relationship to Christ in personal experience. Some Christians are too self-oriented to be effective as representatives of Christ.

Their only concern is, "What will people think of me?" Theirs is a self-image problem. Those thus concerned have insufficient identification with Christ and His purpose. God has ordained that those who follow Christ should be image-bearers, not image-builders![6] He desires that they be concerned about what they *are* in Christ, not what people can be caused to *think* they are outside of Him. Believers are to become like Christ, to reflect Him, to witness to Him.[7] If they do, they will not "faint." Fear fades in the face of a personal revelation of Jesus Christ . . . and faith comes.

Fear also results from the lack of a working knowledge of the Word of God, a lack of preparation. Too many Christians do not know sufficiently the Biblical basis of their salvation. Some even have doubts and questions, themselves. They do not know the facts of redemption. They have not "searched" the Scriptures. As a result they cannot share their belief.

How can this fear-guilt cycle be broken? How can believers get started? The solution does not lie simply in "preaching people under conviction," in making them feel guiltier, hoping they will break out of fear and go! The solution will be found when believers truly place Christ at the center of their lives; in a cleansing from sin, in prayer and the infilling of the Holy Spirit, in study of the Word of God, in experience and action.

PLACE CHRIST AT THE CENTER

Christ is not only Saviour; He is Lord! He can accept no second place. He cannot confront sinners through His followers unless they follow Him in every sense of the Word, unless He sits in the "throne room!"

As the disciples followed Jesus, they eventually learned that this meant more than accepting Him as the Messiah; it meant the absolute surrender of one's whole life to Him, an acceptance of His Sovereignty. There was a cross involved in following Him.[8] Supreme love demanded complete obedience. "If ye love me ye will keep my commandments."[9]

SEEK CLEANSING FROM SIN

The Christian who would become a soul winner must free himself from unconfessed sin and live in victory. How? Read 1 John 1:7, 9. Nothing will short-circuit the power of God in one's life and inhibit the working of the Holy Spirit like the residue of unconfessed sin. The Christian whose conscience is dealing with him will hardly be able to deal with a sinner. The first, and only, message of the Spirit he will hear is the message of conviction concerning his own need.

PRAY AND BE FILLED WITH THE HOLY SPIRIT

The Early Church knew how to deal with the fear problem! They knew what first broke the fear cycle for them and what would continue to do so. Their dynamic witness was born in the outpouring of the Holy Spirit as they waited in prayer.[10] When confronted by the Sanhedrin, Peter showed no fear, and "filled with the Holy Ghost, said . . . be it known . . . that by the name of Jesus Christ . . . this man doth stand here."[11] When the Sanhedrin "threatened the disciples they returned to the company of believers and together prayed for boldness." They were "all filled with the Holy Ghost, and they spake the Word of God with boldness . . . And with great power gave the apostles witness."[12]

Prayer and the infilling of the Holy Spirit are the

Biblical answer to fear! Throughout The Acts this is the pattern. In writing to the young man, Timothy, the Apostle Paul stated "Stir up the gift . . . for God hath not given us a spirit of fear, but of power, and of love, and of a sound mind. Be not thou therefore ashamed of the testimony of our Lord."[13]

STUDY THE WORD AND PREPARE

Believers need to be *armed* with the Word. They need to *work in it* in discussion with fellow believers. They need to vocalize their beliefs and understandings, to ask questions and seek answers about the doctrine of salvation. They need exercise in the use of the Word. They need "Word Power!" The Sword must become a familiar weapon in their hands!

Bible study and preparation includes these steps:

1. *Secure a New Testament.* Mark the selected salvation Scripture verses to use in soul winning. Carry it always!

2. *Think and rethink the salvation Scripture verses.* Read and reread them; meditate upon them! Become so familiar with them that all hesitancy is gone in their use.

3. *Discuss the Scripture verses,* the approaches, the comments to make, with fellow believers. Find a soul-winning partner with whom soul-winning development can occur interactively.

4. *Engage in lab sessions. Practice!* This may seem strange at first. It will become enjoyable. Nothing has done more to get soul winners started than practice with friends in an acceptance situation. A lab session involves making an approach to a "prospect" and following through in conversation in a wide variety of "situations." One person becomes the "prospect" while two others call on him as soul-winning partners. One partner takes the lead, makes an approach and follows through as the "prospect" reponds. When the conversation ends, workers change roles and try again. Afterwards they constructively rethink the efforts for added learning, and an instructor guides to more effective work.

5. *"Go" looking for a prospect, a "harvest."*[14] The Holy Spirit will lead! After preliminary preparation, it is best to learn by doing.

One can grow going! As the young eagle must be made to try his wings, Christians must be sent.

This was precisely the method Jesus employed in training His disciples. He demonstrated soul winning in real-life laboratory situations. Then, when His disciples had learned enough to get started, He sent them out. Jesus knew that in order for learning to be complete it must involve personal experience. Observation-knowledge would not be enough; action-experience must follow!

Jesus did not force His disciples to go until they were ready. But as soon as they had enough to get started He sent them forth.[15] He understood that they had much more to learn. They would need more instruction when they returned. But after this He would send them again and again. Thus in action-training they would bridge the gap between themselves and the world, breaking the fear barrier in a natural way, and they would learn by doing.

It is significant to notice that, after sending His disciples out, Jesus also went! He did not ask them to do something He did not do. He never ceased being an example.

6. *Study the doctrine of salvation.* The soul winner who is in earnest will desire to learn all he can about the great truths of redemption. He will continue to "search" the Scriptures and to learn more about God's way of reconciliation. Proficiency in soul winning will come through this continuous cycle of study and action.

JESUS AND THE APPROACH

The effort to open a soul-winning conversation is referred to as the *approach.* The effort to turn a conversation and direct it toward spiritual things and God is referred to as the *transition.* Each of these areas poses problems and therefore merits special study. Mature soul winners constantly restudy these two areas looking for improvement. First, we will consider the approach from the point of view of Jesus, The Master Soul Winner. Then we will consider two basic approaches and finally transition.

An ideal concept of approach was expressed by Dr. Myron A. Augsburger. He stated: "The approach is not to buttonhole each person and preach a young sermon, but to seek in normal dialog to express the

joy of life in Christ in such a way as to capture the
other man's interest and communicate an invitation to
faith."[16] In this light Paul's attitude, ". . . I am made
all things to all men, that I might by all means save
some" appears ideal.[17]

THE APPROACHES JESUS USED

It is helpful to notice the manner in which Jesus
effected approach. He employed both direct and indirect approaches. However, for Him, the approach
was often made by the prospect. Even His presence
elicited contact and called for His response. The "people sought him out" and desired to hear what He
had to say.[18]

Notice the approaches Jesus made to four individuals:
In the case of the Samaritan woman (John 4), Jesus'
approach was indirect in that He asked for a drink.
However, the essence of His transition to spiritual
water was contained in His approach. Zacchaeus (Luke
19) came "to see," but Jesus made the approach. It
was indirect—"I must abide at thy house." However,
it too had the elements of the transition in it—"this
day is salvation come to this house." In the case of
Nathaniel (John 1), Jesus used honest commendation,
indirectly startling Nathaniel and then leading him
to a confession of faith. In Peter's case (John 1:42;
Matt. 4:19), it was Andrew who brought him to Jesus.
Jesus' first approach to Peter, however, was direct
and spiritual—"Thou art . . . thou shalt be. . . ." His
second approach on the seashore likewise was direct
—"Follow me." The seed of prophetic utterance had
lodged in Peter's heart from the first contact. When
the second approach came, he was "ready."

THE INSTRUCTIONS JESUS GAVE

It is significant also to notice what Jesus told His disciples to say when He sent them out.

1. *To the twelve* (Matt. 10). Jesus gave them a specific subject to discuss—"The Kingdom of heaven is at hand." It almost appears this was to be the opening line of their preaching and conversations. Certainly they were to turn to this subject as soon as possible. It was a direct, spiritual approach.

2. *To the seventy* (Luke 10). As Jesus instructed them, He indicated "into whatsoever house" they entered they were to say: "Peace be to this house." This was an approach much in keeping with greetings of the day, an indirect approach. And yet, it contained within it a ready-made opportunity for transition—peace.

3. *Following the resurrection.* Of interest, too, are the instructions Jesus gave at various occasions after His resurrection.[19] In these different appearances Jesus returned to the general instructions and the charge to "go." He said nothing specific about the approach they were to make. However, implied was the fact that *they* were to make the approach and, it would seem, it must be quite direct. They were to "go," and to "make disciples," to preach "repentance and remission of sins." Also, they were to go *"as"* He had come. They were to do what they had seen Him do.

TWO BASIC TYPES OF APPROACH

At this point our study turns to personal evangelism which has as its object the winning of individuals right where they are, whether it be in door-to-door contact or in chance opportunities which occur. It concerns soul winners who deliberately get themselves involved in contact with others in order to witness.

In general the two basic types of approach already alluded to are used in such efforts—indirect and direct. The indirect seeks to use what is at hand as an "opener" and plans to turn the conversation at the opportune moment. It starts the conversation slowly and sometimes on a theme quite oblique to the theme of spiritual things and then watches for an opening. The direct approach seeks to open and turn the conversation to spiritual things at the same time.

It should be noted that it is not the artfulness of the approach that is relied on to win. No approach can "guarantee" results! Rather, the approach is simply the means of opening a conversation in such a way as to lead to an opportunity in which seed can be sowed and/or a harvest reaped.

THE INDIRECT APPROACH

The indirect approach begins where people are—their interests, concerns, likes, family, home occupation, hobbies—and seeks to escalate the conversation. Thus, the starting point may be any one of a thousand things. The indirect type approach has been used both in every-day and in door-to-door witnessing.

1. *In every-day witnessing.* A casual conversation which may occur any one of many places can suddenly become a very meaningful conversation. It can be opened and pursued with such questions as these: "How long have you lived here? Where do you work, or what is your occupation? What is 'home' to you?" And more direct, "What church do you attend? What would you say is the basic spiritual need of people today?" The average "prospect" often will turn the conversation and ask the "worker" to express his views.

At that moment an opportunity may come to turn the conversation to spiritual things or for a word of testimony.

The two key techniques to observe in the indirect approach are: (1) *the worker encourages the prospect to talk about himself* and (2) *he gradually leads the conversation.* Thus the worker has opportunity to learn just what the status, need, attitudes, and thoughts of the prospect are; and he discovers a basis for the pursuit of a soul-winning conversation. Also, he has opportunity to establish rapport, confidence, and understanding. Occasionally a "continuing" conversation may develop out of such an approach, a conversation that may take days or even weeks to mature.

Another form of every-day indirect approach is found in the use of various devices such as lapel pins, both fish hooks and question marks. Also, various desk top "witnesses" have been employed. These objects being prominently in view quite naturally provide openings in the business situation and in every-day life.

2. *In door-to-door contact and street evangelism.* Various indirect approaches have been used in this type evangelism as well. Always the worker remains sensitive to the leading of the Holy Spirit and watches for the opening. More recent "door-to-door" efforts have included: the survey, the census, the literature "sowdown," and the "get acquainted" visit. The opinion poll has been used effectively, among college-age young people, as a bridge to a witnessing conversation. Its primary purpose is to sample opinion on religious questions. It starts young people thinking in a spiritual direction.

THE DIRECT APPROACH

The current burden to win souls which many carry calls for a very deliberate kind of contact. It is an approach in keeping with the purpose and spirit of this kind of "going."

The direct approach assumes the Holy Spirit is working and that gospel seed has been sown. It seeks to work with the Holy Spirit and to follow His leading both in finding the harvest and in reaping it. Various approaches of a very direct nature have been used with success, such as these:

1. "We're concerned about our nation and are out talking to people about spiritual things, or we're out asking people what they think about it."

2. "Hi! I dare say you can't guess what we're doing"—used by young people. When the "prospect" responds, the worker follows with a direct statement of spiritual conversation purpose.

3. "My name is _____. This is my friend, _____. We're a couple of men out talking to people about Jesus Christ. What do you think about a thing like that?"

4. "I owe you an apology. I've lived in this neighborhood two years and have never told you what Jesus has done for me."

5. Literature "door openers" have been found very effective. They are usually quite direct, having the plan of salvation printed in them. Often Scripture texts are accompanied by simple illustrations which help convey the message. If interest is shown, the literature tool becomes the conversation piece, and its "steps" are followed in pointing the individual to Christ. If interest is mild—no "harvest" is ready—then the worker seeks to leave it with the prospect as "seed" with a prayer that interest and conviction will ensue.

Variety in approach seems to be the earmark of all direct soul-winning efforts. Workers are constantly rethinking the ones they use and looking for improvement. Each person must be himself and be natural. Any sense of "memorized" or "learned" approach will raise a barrier. Ease and spontaneity will lower barriers and invite response. A smile, friendliness, warmth, and radiant Christian faith will help bridge the gap and provide rapport. The person who likes people and wants to win them, who has a vital experience and is eager to share it, will find a way!

EFFECTING TRANSITION

The point in the conversation at which the soul winner senses he can conveniently turn the conversation to spiritual things is called transition. As a rule, this should be a natural "turn," just as conversations might turn.

It is interesting to notice how Jesus effected transition in various conversations. In dealing with Nicodemus, Jesus immediately sensed his need and abruptly turned the conversation—"Verily, verily, I say . . ." In the case of the rich young ruler, Jesus used questions and answers, probing the expression of the young man and directing his thought.[20] In the case of the lawyer Jesus again turned the conversation by using questions related to what the lawyer had said.[21] In working with the woman of Samaria Jesus used a direct, startling statement that grew out of his approach.[22] He turned the conversation from natural water to spiritual water.

KEY PRINCIPLES OF TRANSITION

The first key principle to observe in working for transition is this: *Let the prospect talk! Listen carefully to what he says and use it.* By using leading questions and engaging him in dialogue the worker has a chance to "read" the thoughts, desires, and needs of the prospect. He will get a sense of his spiritual state and a sense of direction for further conversation.

As the worker listens he will find answers to such

questions as these: "Has he allowed the Holy Spirit to work in his life at all? Does he have basic Bible knowledge? What is his spiritual status? Is he resentful? Is he open? Is there an immediate need in his life?" The Holy Spirit will provide discernment and lead the worker in such a moment. Many soul winners have thrilled at being "taught" just what to say in such a moment.

The second key principle in transition is: *Move the conversation towards the need expressed or sensed.* It may be a need for a decision, for prayer, for more Bible knowledge or an explanation of salvation. It may be the worker senses the prospect needs to be related to a church or simply will need time to think. Perhaps he needs a promise of a further visit, an offer of help, or simply a promise to pray for him. (However, it is easy to yield to the temptation to promise prayer when a more direct and continued confrontation is needed.) Once the worker turns the conversation toward the immediate need, he will "stick with it" and pursue his purpose.

KEY QUESTIONS TO USE

Key questions have been used effectively in transition. Questions have strategic value in keeping a conversation moving. They have value, too, in actually controlling the conversation while at the same time keeping the prospect talking. Experienced soul winners have found that to memorize and hold ready a patterned sequence of questions prepares them for any eventuality. Variations of the following have been used extensively:

1. *"Have you given much thought to spiritual things?"*

2. *"Have you considered becoming a Christian?"*

3. *"If I (someone) were to ask you what a Christian is, what would you say?"* (The use of "someone" brings a "third party" into the conversation. Hence the question is less direct.)

These three questions should be locked in the memory for ready use at any time. They can be adapted to almost any conversation. The latter of the three usually elicits a response about "what a Christian *does.*" This response, itself, is a key bit of information for the soul winner. It should not be rejected with a "no." The question can be repeated with stress on *"is."*[23]

4. *Have you had a personal experience with Jesus Christ, or are you on the way?"* The value of this question lies in its direct expression of the nature of the new birth. A prospect will not reply "yes" unless he knows what is meant and has had an experience. On the other hand, if he does not know or has not had an experience, he has been given an easy alternative—"I guess you could say I'm on the way." This quickly gives the soul winner a sense of spiritual basis and provides an excellent foundation for further conversation.

5. *"Has anyone ever introduced Jesus to you?"* Such a question would be used in a permissive conversation but likewise would lay foundation for further conversation. A "no" answer would naturally follow with the question, "Would you let me introduce Him to you?" Or with a personal testimony.

A special note regarding one question is in order—"Are you a Christian?" Experienced soul winners carefully avoid its use. Too often individuals answer "yes" because they are in a "Christian nation," or "isn't everyone?" To receive a "yes" response to this question can leave the worker greatly handicapped when he has real reason to doubt the prospect's grasp of what a Christian is.

KEY STATEMENTS TO USE

Direct statements can also be used in effecting transition. Such statements as these, by way of example, show what can be done:

1. "I'm glad to see your interest in (*whatever prospect's concern is*). I believe that Christ can help you. I'd like to discuss becoming a Christian with you."

2. "I appreciate your sincerity. I think you would make a good Christian just like the Apostle Paul. I'd like to talk to you about it."

3. "Regardless of (*whatever has transpired in prospect's life*), I want you to know God loves you. That is why I'm here talking with you in this way. It could well be God brought us together..."

Thus far we have considered the soul-winning encounter up through the point of transition. The next point of consideration is the soul-winning conversation itself, the presentation of the plan of salvation.

CHAPTER 7

GUIDING THE SOUL-WINNING CONVERSATION

. . . EXPLAINING THE PLAN OF SALVATION

At this point in our study, it is assumed that the transition to spiritual things has been effected in the conversation. The prospect is interested. Hence, attention is now turned first to several general soul-winning action-principles, then to six basic principles to observe in presenting salvation, and finally to a sample soul-winning conversation.

GENERAL ACTION PRINCIPLES

These general action principles apply in any soul-winning encounter. They affect the approach and transition, the presentation of salvation's plan and the "closing" of a decision for Christ. It will be helpful to study them at this point.

RADIATE LOVE—IT COMMUNICATES

What prospective soul winner has not approached a home with fear and trembling only to find the love of Christ overshadows his ineffectiveness and blunders? The soul winner needs this inner glow. It comes from a vital relationship with Christ through the Holy Spirit and grows by continuous contact with the unsaved.

A simple personal testimony which radiates this love will have a profound effect upon the unsaved. All soul winning starts in love!

BE A GOOD LISTENER

Every individual wants an audience. It is courteous and complimentary to pay attention to your host. Rapport can be developed in no better way. By listening carefully to your host, you will also have opportunity to evaluate him and find the point of contact that will produce spiritual concern.

LEARN THE ATTENTION PRINCIPLE

A fundamental principle in soul winning is that you must get the prospect's attention and then focus it on spiritual things. If you try to stir a glass of water with a pencil, you will notice that the water does not turn all at once. It gradually begins to follow the track of the pencil. So it is with the minds of men. It is important to focus the attention of their minds. This takes time. Furthermore, the focus of attention is not forced; it is led.

KEEP YOUR WEAPONS HIDDEN

Carry a New Testament, not a Bible. To "brandish the sword" puts your host on the defensive. Proverbs 1:17 says, "Surely in vain the net is spread in the sight of any bird." The New Testament should have clear print and should be small enough to fit into a woman's purse or a man's shirt or coat pocket. (NOTE: See instructions for marking your Testament, page 111). You will also need select salvation tracts and helps for new converts.

HAVE A BASIC PLAN FOR SOUL WINNING

It is not necessary that everyone use the same Scripture verses, but it is important that all soul winners seek to cooperate with the Holy Spirit on certain basic steps of soul winning. Having a plan helps inexperienced soul winners feel confident about what to say next; experienced soul winners use a plan as if it were second nature.

BE RELAXED

The soul winner must have a relaxed, joyful spirit. This helps put the prospect at ease. A relaxed spirit comes from:

1. *Prayer.* A consistent prayer life results in right motives and total dependence upon the Holy Spirit, which in turn helps the worker to relax.

2. *Knowledge.* A worker will have confidence to witness if he has a thorough knowledge of soul-winning principles and Scripture verses.

3. *Practice.* Everyone is apprehensive at first; however, a few engagements will soon reveal that the Holy Spirit makes up for personal lack.

WORK TOGETHER IN "TWOS" WHEN POSSIBLE

Soul winners find it advantageous to go two by two. Jesus recognized the value of this principle and "sent" the disciples this way. Each worker has his assigned responsibility. It is a soul winner's responsibility to make the approach and lead the conversation. It is the associate's responsibility to:

1. *Pray.*

2. *Listen carefully.*

3. *Give a personal testimony when it is needed.* He acts as a reinforcement. He should not interrupt but should sense when his help is needed and be ready to respond when the leader calls for help.

4. *Assist as needed.* The associate should take charge of such details as seating the soul winner and the prospect together, entertaining any children, watching for and deflecting any interference, and taking charge of any emergency.

WITNESS TO ONE PERSON AT A TIME

Where two or more individuals are encountered, eliminate the possibility of sidetracks by dealing with one person at a time. Choose the dominant member of the group, such as a father or a husband. When you come to the point of accepting Christ, simply ask the other individual or individuals if they would be willing to bow their heads and accept Christ as their Saviour too. Experience has shown that usually the second person will follow the one who is leading the way.

NEVER ARGUE

To argue is to lose everything. You do not have to agree with all that is said, but you can avoid arguings by such comments as: "That's a thought"; "That's one view"; or "Perhaps we can discuss that another night."

AVOID A DISCUSSION OF CHURCH ASSOCIATION OR DOCTRINE

The mention of church membership or even making church attendance the focal point of your opening conversation presents two serious problems. First, to many, church membership and salvation are synonymous. Consequently, if you stress these subjects, your prospect may conclude that being a "good church member" is all he needs to do to be saved.

Second, you can be put in the position of proselyting. Most people associate themselves with some religious group whether or not they attend regularly. Any conversation relative to church membership will cause him to retreat to this religious association.

CONTROL THE INTERRUPTIONS

Interruptions can come at the most inopportune times. Often these are hindrances of Satan. The telephone, noisy children, neighbors, and an interrupting companion. Many of the interruptions can be overcome by an alert associate. In some cases, it is necessary for the soul winner to cheerfully pause and wait for the situation to change. Don't fret; often during these interruptions the Holy Spirit is continuing His work. Use the time to pray, to bind every hindering spirit. Then simply continue at the opportune time.

RELY ON THE AUTHORITY OF THE WORD

Many times in witnessing, an individual will say, "I don't believe that," or, "Are you sure?" Don't let a statement such as this bother you. He's not arguing with you but with God. Don't defend the Word of God. There's power and authority in it. Simply use it! It takes time for the Holy Spirit to break through to the individual's heart. Often the same individual who says he does not believe the Bible will later break under the compelling power of the Word.

DON'T TRY TO FORCE THE HARVEST

There's a difference between resistance and resentment. Each prospect displays a certain amount of resistance. This can be broken by the Holy Spirit driving the Word into his heart. Resentment is another matter. If you detect this, you will realize the harvest is not ripe. Break off the conversation courteously, hoping for a future opportunity when the harvest has

developed. Prayerfully leave a piece of literature and
remember a seed has been sown.

SALVATION CONVERSATION PRINCIPLES

Basic principles guide the soul winner in working
with the Holy Spirit and in using the Word to bring
a soul to Christ. Six such basic principles are given.
Scripture verses other than the ones suggested may be
used. The important thing, however, is to learn the
basic principles and to follow them in unfolding the
truth which becomes the basis for salvation.

THE PROSPECT MUST KNOW GOD LOVES HIM

The sinner must get a revelation of God's love in
giving His Son. God proved His love by His Gift.
Only the Holy Spirit can fully reveal this truth, but
the soul winner can lay the foundation for understanding through John 3:16, which reveals these truths:

1. God loves the sinner.

2. The proof of His love is that He gave His only
Son to die on the cross.

3. God did this so the sinner might escape his inevitable destiny of separation from God.

4. God's free gift is everlasting life.

THE PROSPECT MUST WEIGH THE COST OF REJECTING CHRIST

Can you recall what prompted you to turn your attention toward salvation? Sometime or other you were
made aware of where you were headed after death.
You must have weighed the cost of accepting Christ
against the cost and consequences of rejecting Him.
Your need outweighed the cost, so you accepted Christ
as your Saviour.

The story of the rich man in Luke 16:19-25 graphically illustrates the cost of rejection. Read it prayer-

fully and carefully until the following facts grip you.

1. *There are two types of people.* The first is rich in desires for the pleasures of this present life, giving little attention to the next life. The other spends considerable time and substance planning and working for the next life. (This would be true regardless of his financial status in life. His real pleasures and ambition are in the life to come.) Every person is in one class or the other.

2. *Both classes of people will die.*

3. *The rich man died and went to hell.* He lifted up his eyes and cried out asking for someone to dip his fingers in water and cool his tongue. In the life to come people will have a body with faculties to feel and see. Think of spending eternity in this horrible place of torment. In using this story make your description live in vivid detail until your prospect can see himself there. Be very careful, however, not to arouse resentment by giving him the impression that you are placing him there. Let him classify himself. You are only presenting him the Word of God. He will conclude that everyone is going there who has not accepted God's plan of salvation. Don't become involved in whether or not this story is a parable. Jesus told it with the definite purpose of warning every individual to escape such an awful place.

THE PROSPECT MUST SEE THAT HE CHOOSES HIS OWN DESTINY

Sinners often comment that they cannot imagine a righteous God sending an individual to such a place. This is a perfect opening to refer again to John 3:16 and stress that each man's choice determines his destiny. You may also wish to refer to Hebrews 2:3, "How shall we escape if we neglect so great salvation." Emphasize that "we" is all-inclusive; every man must choose. Emphasize the main word "neglect." It is not a matter of total rejection of God, it is simply neglecting to receive what God has offered. God does not send anyone to hell. The person who neglects God's offer literally sends himself to hell.

THE PROSPECT MUST SEE THAT HE MUST TURN FROM SIN

This is repentance. No man can be saved unless he *turns* from sin to God. The Holy Spirit presses the claims of Christ on the sinner. The sinner must turn and accept. When Peter had preached and the crowd was convicted, they cried, "What shall we do?" Peter replied, "Repent, and be baptized everyone of you in the name of Jesus Christ for the remission of sin." (NOTE: An amplified discussion of repentance and its relation to the conclusion of the soul-winning conversation is contained in the next chapter.)

THE PROSPECT MUST SEE THE IMPORTANCE OF RECEIVING CHRIST

John 1:12 may be used to reveal this truth. It is important here to show the difference between believing and receiving. It is possible for a person to believe the entire plan of salvation without having appropriated it by an act of faith.

The key word in John 1:12 is "receive." It may help to illustrate this important principle. You might suggest to your prospect, "Just pretend this card is a twenty-dollar bill and I tell you it is yours if you will take it. You can believe it is yours, but it never will be until you reach out and take it." At this point get him to take it out of your hand. By this simple act of appropriation, the difference between believing and receiving can be illustrated graphically.

THE PROSPECT MUST BE SHOWN HOW TO RECEIVE CHRIST

Revelation 3:20 graphically illustrates this. "Behold I stand at the door and knock, if any man opens unto me, I will come in." Stop at this point. The need is to present the truth of our power to choose. Show the prospect that the God of the universe can do anything except force His way into an individual's life.

Draw a word picture of Christ, standing, waiting, knocking over and over, asking to come in. Draw the prospect's attention to the various circumstances of his life. In these, Christ has been endeavoring to gain access into his life.

At this point the sinner may weigh the cost of accepting Christ as his Saviour against the tragedy of rejecting God's wonderful gift. The soul winner must believe the Holy Spirit will reveal to the sinner the simplicity of opening his heart's door in an act of faith and inviting Jesus to come in. Remember, this is not your battle; it is God's. The Holy Spirit will do His work effectively.

A Sample Salvation Conversation

By learning to apply these six principles in the proper sequence, the soul winner will lead his prospect to an assuring and abiding faith in Christ. All previous approach and conversation with the prospect has been groundwork for this most important message. A plan of action can be shown best in a sample salvation conversation.

Several different Scriptural series can be used in leading a sinner to Christ. The essential thing is to work with the Holy Spirit and observe the basic principles outlined. A typical conversation may illustrate the use of Scripture passages and these basic principles.

(NOTE: You are now at the point in conversation where the approach and transition have been effected. If you are invited to or find it opportune, use your New Testament in presenting the plan of salvation.)

STEP 1: INTRODUCE THE SINNER TO THE GOD OF LOVE

Scripture: John 3:16, "For God so loved the world, that he gave his only begotten Son, that whosoever believeth in him should not perish, but have everlasting life."

YOUR COMMENT: "One of the most familiar Scripture verses in the Bible, John 3:16, reveals what God thinks of you and me. It reveals further what God has done so that you can make the right choice of your eternal destiny today."

(NOTE: Remember, the true power of drawing a sinner to Christ is your life radiating the love of God for that individual unsaved person. The Holy Spirit will breathe upon this Scripture verse and through your lips will make the love of God real to him.)

"The phrase, 'for God so loved,' lays bare the heart, of God and reveals the depth of His feelings for you. Notice the object of His love, 'the world.' The proof of His love is in the phrase 'gave his only begotten Son.' What could there be that God is trying to keep us from that would make Him love us so much as to give His Son? You'll notice it in these words, 'should not perish, but have everlasting life.' I don't know of any one of us who would unhesitatingly give his boy or girl for any cause in this world, but God gave His only Son to suffer and to die on Calvary's cross. There must be a great reason why He gave His Son to die for you."

STEP 2: SHOW THE UNSAVED THE HORRIBLE DESTINY AWAITING SINNERS WHO REJECT GOD'S LOVE

Scripture: Luke 16:19-25 (NOTE: You may not want to read all the verses. It would be better to become thoroughly familiar and tell the story in your own language in modern terms.)

YOUR COMMENT: "There's a story in the Bible that reveals vividly what it means to perish. You find it in Luke 16:19-25. Let me briefly tell you this story. Two men were living side by side. One was a rich man. His house was full of servants; he had the nicest lawn in town, the finest of homes, the best of furniture, and the finest of food. He had everything a man could desire. A poor man lived at his gate. The poor man spent his time begging a few crumbs of bread to keep himself alive. There was nothing wrong with the rich man's having all these things except that his only objective in life was his possessions.

"Each man was destined to die, just as we are. Money could not buy the rich man any more time. Notice their destination. The poor man went to heaven, the rich man went to hell. Here is the most vivid description in the Bible of what it is like in hell. The rich man lifted up his eyes, cried out, asking for someone to dip his fingers in water and cool his burning tongue and lips. The story indicates that in the next life we will have a body with the ability to feel, see, and think. Imagine an individual spending a year in such a place as that—but this is for eternity."

(NOTE: Don't be afraid to speak of hell. Remember, the Word of God says that anyone who rejects God's divine provision is going there. It's God's Word, not yours. Don't be sidetracked at this point. The individual may state he believes it's only a parable. Don't argue. Simply state that even if it were a parable, it would not change the truth of the story. Stay on target. Exchange ideas without arguing. Your prospect will consider the possibility of your thought.)

"Just think, we will have a body with feeling. How awful it would be to be in a place like hell."

(NOTE: By this time, the prospect will be doing some serious thinking. Drive home his responsibility.

"Would you like to go to a place like that? Would you want to be responsible for your wife and children spending eternity in such a place?"

(NOTE: His likely answer will be: "I can't imagine a loving God putting an individual in such a place as this." The Holy Spirit is beginning to do His work. Agree with him.)

"I can't either. As a matter of fact, God doesn't put a person there; a person puts himself there by neglecting God's divine provision revealed in John 3: 16. God wants you to escape going to such a place so much that He gave His Son to die so you would not have to go. Would you want to turn your back upon God's provision for you to escape a place like that?"

Prospect's answers may vary. "No, I wouldn't." Or, "I don't think I'm such a sinner." Or, "I don't think I'm going to a place like that."

(Remember, this is not a religious argument. The Holy Spirit will do His work of convicting. You may want to refer to Hebrews 2:3, pinpointing the word "neglect." "How shall we escape, if we neglect so great salvation." The rich man went to hell because he neglected to accept God's divine provision.)

STEP 3: SHOW THE SINNER THAT HE MUST RECEIVE CHRIST TO BE SAVED

Scripture verse: John 1:12, "But as many as received him, to them gave he power to become the sons of God, even to them that believe on his name."

YOUR COMMENT: "You will notice one oustanding word in this verse. 'Receive.' Many people believe God has provided for their salvation, but this word is not 'believe'; it is 'receive.' "

(NOTE: Take a bill from your wallet to illustrate this.)

"Here's a dollar bill. You can believe I have it for you. I could tell you if you would take this dollar, it would be yours. You could believe it all you wanted to, but it wouldn't be yours until you received it. There are many who believe God has a plan of salvation who have never reached out to take it. Go ahead and take it out of my hand." (As he reaches for it, you suggest:) "Now it's yours, but why?"

SUBJECT: "Because I took it."

(You can break any tension here by reaching out and taking it out of his hand and suggesting:)

"See, as long as it was in my hand, it wasn't yours; but when you reached out and took it, then you appropriated it."

(NOTE: This visual can graphically illustrate the difference between believing and receiving. Any object can be used to illustrate this point. Suddenly, the reality of action between believing and receiving will become apparent to him.)

"Let me show you one more Scripture verse. It shows how we can reach out by faith and receive Jesus Christ."

STEP 4: SHOW THE SINNER HOW HE MAY RECEIVE SALVATION

Scripture verse: Revelation 3:20, "Behold I stand at the door, and knock: if any man hear my voice, and open the door, I will come in to him." (NOTE: Stop at this point and do not continue further. The remainder of the verse does not add to your purpose.)

YOUR COMMENT: (Believe the Holy Spirit will reveal the truth of what is involved in rejecting or accepting Christ in this graphic illustration.)

"Consider the God of the universe who made all the stars in the heavens. He made the smallest things in His creation perfect in their order. The smallest bit of matter is majestic in its concept, all created by our wonderful God. Can you see the majestic Son of God standing humbly before the door of your heart for you to open it for Him?"

(NOTE: Perhaps you'd like to make reference to Sallman's picture of Christ, revealing Christ before the door, the handle on the inside. The obvious reason, Christ does not force himself into anyone's life.)

"That door is controlled by your will. God gave His Son to die for you, to keep you from going to the awful place called hell. It is a matter of your choice whether you will open the door or not. He stands there now, knocking and knocking, waiting for an invitation to come in."

(NOTE: You may wish to tap him on the shoulder or knock on a close object to drive home this point. You could refer to some circumstances that he has cited before to illustrate that Christ is using many ways to reach him.)

"You have a free will; God will not violate it. He will not force your heart's door open even though He has all power. As your friend, if I would come upon your porch and stand there knocking, you would look out and see me there, what would you say to me?" (His obvious answer:) "Come in."

(NOTE: Experience has shown many times the unsaved will use the words "Come in, of course," illustrating the logic of this illustration. This is the time to breathe a prayer and to believe for the power to break the chains of sin. Carefully pursue the subject.)

"I'm not the one doing the knocking today. It is God's Son who in love comes to you through the power of the Holy Spirit. It is God's time for you to open the door of your life and simply invite Him to come in."

By developing and learning one's own conversational plan, the soul winner will be more capable of leading the conversation to its desired end. Whenever questions or problems might tend to sidetrack the conversation from its main objective, the worker may more easily return to his plan and direct the sinner to a decision.

Through the application of these action soul-winning principles in a planned conversation, it is possible for the soul winner to direct any person to Jesus Christ. When these principles are thoroughly understood and the conversation plan learned, they will go far toward freeing the soul winner from the fear of man. In fact, he will have a great confidence in the power of the Holy Spirit to convict the sinner through the Word and testimony, and thus to bring him to a positive decision for Christ.

In the next chapter we will discuss the final part of the soul-winning conversation, which includes leading the sinner to accept Christ and helping him find assurance of salvation.

CHAPTER 8

CLOSING THE SOUL-WINNING CONVERSATION

. . . DECISION AND ASSURANCE

Many Christians witness for Christ, but too few follow through to a point of praying with the prospect and helping him actually accept Christ as Saviour. The most common reason is a lack of ability to close the witness by helping the prospect make an immediate decision. It is like hooking a fish but being unable to land it.

There is also the need for building assurance. What do you say when you have seen someone fervently seek the Lord and you ask, "Do you know you are saved?" and he answers, "No, I'm really not sure." Very likely this person is looking to his feelings and needs to be instructed more fully.

We shall discuss in this chapter the basic conditions of salvation, the closing salvation conversation, and what we can do besides praying to bring assurance to the sincere seeker.

Providing an Understanding of Salvation

Most people agree that Christ has brought salvation to man, but many differ about how salvation may be obtained. Just how does one obtain salvation? We must look to the Bible for the answer. When Paul was traveling from Asia to Jerusalem, he stopped by to instruct the Ephesian elders. In the course of his discussion he explained that he had been "testifying both to the Jews, and also to the Greeks, repentance toward God, and faith toward our Lord Jesus Christ."[1] Here we have clearly stated the two requirements for salvation: repentance toward God and faith toward Christ. No one can be saved without meeting these conditions.

REPENTANCE TOWARD GOD

Repentance is often neglected in our dealings with men. Yet it was emphasized by John the Baptist, Jesus, and the Apostles. Jesus said, "Except ye repent, ye shall . . . perish."[2] It is his first step toward God. In repentance, a man faces the responsibility of his sin. First, we settle the question of sin; then we can bring faith into action. This is the order Jesus implied in Matthew 21:32, "Ye repented not . . . that ye might believe." Men need to mourn over their sin, to be sorry for offending God.

Repentance is genuine only if we are willing to *confess* our sins to Christ and *forsake* them. But "if we confess our sin, He is faithful and just to forgive us our sin, and to cleanse us from all unrighteousness."[3]

In a soul-winning conversation, it is wise to ask the prospect an open question like this: "How would you explain the meaning of repentance?" This will keep his interest as well as give an opportunity to fill in what he lacks in understanding; but avoid preaching at him.

To awaken his conscience, it may be necessary to use an indirect method: to tell a story like Nathan (2

Samuel 12:3) ; give your personal testimony; or, better yet, have a new convert testify (not preach) ; or give directions, as Christ did in John 4:16.

FAITH TOWARD OUR LORD JESUS CHRIST

Repentance does not save the soul, even though it is essential heart preparation. It is faith that bridges the gap between God and man.

1. *Faith is necessary.* Paul tells us, "By grace are ye saved through faith."[4] It is by faith in the atonement that we may be declared righteous.[5] And Paul also says that being "justified by faith, we have peace with God."[6]

While God is not a respecter of persons, He is a respecter of faith. Regardless of the color of our skin, social standing, or economic status, faith is necessary to bring man into right relationship with God. "Without faith it is impossible to please Him."[7] But faith toward Christ will bring a man into right relationship with God.

God has given every man a measure of faith. It operates in the natural as well as the spiritual. For example, when we purchase a loaf of bread from the bakery, we have confidence that it is bread. We do not analyze its contents or even question the baker; we accept it in faith. Since God is the source of our faith, it seems reasonable that He would require its manifestation in the process of redemption.

The requirement of faith was illustrated in the experience of Philip, the evangelist, who was led by the Spirit to minister to the Eunuch of Ethiopia. He took his text from Isaiah 53 and preached Jesus unto him. The Eunuch responded as soon as he understood, but Philip wisely tested his convert before baptism, and said, "If thou believest with all thine heart, thou mayest." And the Eunuch answered, "I believe."[8]

2. *Faith is reasonable.* William Evans points out, "Faith is no blind act of the soul; it is not a leap in the dark." Faith's foundation is the Word of God, and faith expresses complete trust in the truths contained in the Bible. This includes an absolute faith in the existence of God and that He is a rewarder of them that diligently seek Him.[9]

God's wonderful plan of salvation must be understood if faith is to operate. For example: the prospect must understand that he is a lost sinner and that eternal separation and hell await him as a consequence. He must also understand that while we were yet sinners, Christ died for us so we could be saved from wrath through Him.[10] Faith acts out of understanding.

3. *Faith is action.* Belief is a mental acceptance; faith moves belief into the sphere of action. The individual appropriates for himself the promises of God and takes God at His Word. It is more than faith in a doctrine; it is faith in the Person of the Lord Jesus Christ.

To illustrate faith as a condition of salvation, look to Acts 16:14-31. Paul and Silas were thrown in prison for preaching the gospel. At midnight they were praying and singing praises to God when an earthquake jarred open the prison doors and loosed them from the stocks. The keeper of the prison, trembling with fear, fell down before Paul and Silas with a desperate inquiry, "What must I do to be saved?" They did not have to tell the once proud jail keeper to repent, he was trembling with conviction. They simply said, "Believe on the Lord Jesus Christ, and thou shalt be saved, and thy house."

No matter whom we try to lead to Christ or under what conditions we converse, whether at the altar or in a restaurant, the basic conditions of repentance and faith must be met.

CONFESSION OF CHRIST BEFORE MEN

The person who receives Christ needs to confess his new-found faith immediately. This is natural and necessary, for it is written: "With the heart man believeth unto righteousness; and with the mouth confession is made unto salvation . . . Whosoever believeth on Him shall not be ashamed."[11]

Experienced soul winners have found it wise to encourage the newly saved to "confess Christ" immediately to whoever may be near. This simple act of faith and testimony strengthens conviction, builds assurance, and completes the spiritual transaction.

GUIDING THE CLOSING CONVERSATION AND PRAYER

The soul winner must not only be prepared mentally but spiritually so that he may be sensitive to the leading of the Holy Spirit. At no point is it more essential to work with the Holy Spirit as He works than right here. Be assured that He who has sent us into the whitened harvest field will supply the divine guidance we need at this critical point in the soul winning conversation.

LEADING TO A DECISION BY THE USE OF KEY QUESTIONS

Let us always keep in mind that we are guiding a conversation, not preaching a sermon. The conversation can best be guided the same way a teacher uses questions to draw out answers, telling only what is necessary for complete understanding. The following questions may prove helpful. (Notice that there is no necessary sequence to the suggested questions.)

1. "If I can show you how you can know you are saved, you will do what the Bible says, won't you?" A slight emphasis on the word "know" will help in this question. Usually the prospect will say, "yes," and consequently will feel bound by this word to follow through.

2. "Can you ever remember asking Jesus to forgive you of *your* sins?" Again the reply is the key to the next step to follow. If the answer is in the affirmative, it would be in order to ask: "Do you believe your sins are forgiven now?" In case a negative answer is offered you might suggest that he ask forgiveness for sin at this moment.

3. "If you should die right now would you be ready to meet God?" This is a piercing question and will usually get an honest, straightforward answer, especially, at this point in the discussion. An affirmative answer is not likely and a negative answer opens the opportunity to press for an immediate decision.

4. Sometimes prospects will volunteer that they are lost sinners. Ask the question: "Do you mean to tell me that you are on your way to hell?" When he replies, "yes," then have him describe his understanding of hell. With every word he will indict himself, providing the Holy Spirit with opportunity to convict him even more heavily of sin. By reflecting your understanding of what the prospect said or by repeating the last phrase of his sentence the soul winner can employ listening responses that draw the prospect out. In due time you can suggest a decision that will bring peace in this life and happiness in the life to come.

5. "If your good friend knocked at your door, what would you say to him? (Usually he will respond by saying "come in." Explain this is what Christ is saying in Revelation 3:20, "Behold, I stand at the door, and knock; if any man hear my voice, and open the door, I will come in to him, and will sup with him, and he with me.") As a gentleman, Christ knocks tenderly. He will not force His way into your heart. But with an invitation, He will enter. It is much like inviting in a friend. You must use your voice, lips, words to invite Him in. When you have done your part, He will come in and abide in your heart."

When you use this question technique, your next step will be determined by the prospect's answers. Be careful, even as Christ was in dealing with the Samaritan woman, not to get off on irrelevant matters. Smile, be courteous, and turn the conversation back to the main issue.

EXERCISING AUTHORITY TO BIND THE ENEMY

Soul winners must act in faith and authority. However, this is not the time to preach a sermon in prayer on the doctrine of authority!

An individual who has never been set free by the Lord Jesus is bound by Satan. This is a spiritual battle. The soul winner will sense the powers of darkness reaching to hold their victim. In this moment he must exercise the command of faith through the authority of God's Word and bind the strong man.[12] By this time, if the person is following along, you will be able to take charge and direct the action. For example, you may say, "Let us bow our heads in prayer." More than likely he will close his eyes and bow his head as you call his name in prayer. Then, by the authority invested in you by Christ, loose him from Satan's grip.

Also include in your prayer a petition that your prospect will be saved as he calls on the name of the Lord. The mention of his name, the sincere tone of your voice, and the manifestation of your faith will help him to make his decision and express his faith.

ENCOURAGING THE PENITENT TO PRAY

Before concluding your prayer, stop to give opportunity for the prospect to pray. Encourage him to pray asking forgiveness and inviting Christ into his heart. Instruct him to pray in simple language much as he would talk to his own father. If the person finds it difficult to pray and longer delay seems to embarrass him, simply ask him to repeat a prayer after you something like this: "Dear Jesus, I humbly confess my sins. Come into my heart and make me a child of God. Thank you for saving me right now. In Jesus' Name. Amen."

WITHDRAWAL OF THE SOUL WINNER

There is danger of a prospect's being "won" to a dynamic soul winner and not to Christ. The prospect must have a personal experience with God. Therefore, high pressure tactics must be avoided; and the prospect must be encouraged to pray out of his heart, expressing what he feels. Often at this moment repentant sinners "break" and pour out repentance and contrition before God, experiencing the cleansing of forgiveness.

John the Baptist pointed his followers to Christ and withdrew. "Behold the lamb of God, which taketh away the sin of the world. This is he of whom I said, after me cometh a man which is preferred before me."[13] From his prison cell he restated the matter to inquiring followers: "He must increase, but I must decrease."[14]

Every soul winner should keep in mind that "neither is he that planteth anything, neither he that watereth; but God that giveth the increase."[15]

BUILDING ASSURANCE

Some people confess their sins and accept Christ just as they are instructed to, but for some reason they seem to lack the assurance that should come with receiving Christ. Why? To some the plan of salvation seems too simple; they just can't believe that's all there is to it. Some people may expect an overwhelming emotional experience which does not necessarily occur. What can be done to help them?

1. *Provide understanding based on the Word.* Often doubts persist, even after fervent prayer. Therefore, the convert must be brought back to the infallible Word of God. "Come let us reason together" the Scriptures say. We must *know* the *truth* if it is to set us free. In the parable that Jesus told of the sower and the seed, the good ground represents the one who heareth the word, and understandeth it."[16]

Tears are not enough, the entire personality must be reached—the intellect, the emotions, and the will —if the conversion is to be genuine. "Faith involves the whole of man and has as its object the whole of God's truth."[17] Therefore, keep the proper order in mind: fact, faith, feeling. People expect feelings to motivate faith, but the opposite is true; faith always precedes feelings of joy and peace.

A word of caution is in order. As a rule it is not wise to introduce new Scripture verses at this point. To do so may tend to confuse the seeker. It is better to review the ones already considered. A sample conversation might go something like this:

"John, do you believe you are forgiven?"

"Well, I'm not sure," he replies.

"I can appreciate your honesty, John, but let us look at this Scripture passage again. It says, 'If we confess our sins He is faithful and just to forgive.' In other words, your part is to confess; God's part is to forgive. Since you have sincerely done your part, do you think God would fail to do His part or lie to you?"

To this he may reply, "Oh, no, I can see it now. *I believe*." It may be necessary to have him read the same Scripture verse several times before the light breaks through. "Faith comes by . . . the Word of God."[16]

2. *Use personal testimony to confirm and inspire faith.* A person only possesses what he can express. An experience may be apparent in his radiant countenance or in his actions, but what he says is the most revealing. To draw him out, you might say to him: "John, tell me how you know you are saved." To this he may reply, "Oh, I feel so wonderful." Now this is good, but he needs to be shown that salvation is by faith, not by feeling. He should be equipped with a Bible reason to support his salvation.

It is a paradox—salvation is *kept* by *giving* it to others. To speak of your conversion makes it even more vivid in your mind. As Romans 10:10 says, ". . . with the mouth confession is made unto salvation." In light of this, it would be good to introduce him to a couple of friends to tell each of them how he *knows* he is saved.

Another method of securing an expression of faith

is to enlist the convert to write his testimony on an information card. This often gives you the clearest picture of what has really taken place in his heart.

3. *Encourage him to pray.* There is no substitute for believing prayer. Assurance steals into the heart as God answers and sends the witness of the Holy Spirit.[19] "Build up yourselves on your most holy faith, praying in the Holy Ghost."[20]

When our prayer takes on the added dimension of praise, it becomes a manifestation of faith. To hear a seeker cry out, "Thank You, Jesus, for saving my soul" is the note of victory that is sweet to the ears of the soul winner.

4. *Instruct him to continue in faith.* When Jesus sent forth His apostles to evangelize the world, He did not commission them to secure decisions, but rather to make disciples of all nations. The soul winner to-day does not fulfill his task if he does not keep that goal before him. Therefore, the convert must be taught to continue "steadfastly in the apostles' doctrine and fellowship, and in breaking of bread, and in prayers."[21] This same thought is conveyed in the words of Christ to believing Jews. "Then said Jesus to those Jews which believed on Him, if ye continue in my word, then are ye my disciples indeed."[22]

As the convert follows the teachings of the Word of God, he will grow in the grace and the knowledge of our Lord and Saviour Jesus Christ. His assurance of salvation will build as he learns of Christ's promise, "Because thou hast kept the word . . . I also will keep thee."[23]

THE SOUL WINNER'S CONCLUDING CONVERSATION

"Now, John, that you have accepted Christ as your personal Saviour, you will find life different. The old desires will fade, and you will find new desires entering your heart. The things you used to hate will become precious to you as you let Christ fill your heart with love, peace, and joy. You will find life will be more wonderful and meaningful as you find avenues of service for the Lord.

"Let me warn you, John, that there still will be struggles, problems, and temptations. The big difference is that you now have Christ to help you. 'He that is in you is greater than he that is in the world.'

"Another thing that will strengthen your faith will be to follow the Lord in water baptism. This is an outward sign to the world that Christ has come into your heart and that you are a new creature in Him.

"You should make it a rule of your life to read your Bible and pray daily. Remember you must feed your spiritual life or it will die. In the natural we don't eat one big meal and expect it to sustain us forever; likewise in the spiritual we must feed our souls regularly. I would suggest that you start reading the Gospel of John; and as you read, you will find that the Holy Spirit will open up the Scriptures to you.

"And how about next Sunday, will you meet me at the front door of the church so we can worship together? Fine. Now if you need me, I'm just as close as your telephone.

"Let me again congratulate you for making the most important decision of your life. God bless you."

Marking the New Testament

It is urged that a soul winner carry a New Testament always. This Testament should be marked and ready for instant use. The marking procedure is simple. All that need be done is to select the verses you would like to use, underline them, and key them. It may be desirable to write a brief index in the front of the Testament for ready reference.

In keying the verses just place the reference to the next verse at the bottom of the page or in the margin by the first verse. (The page number where the next verse is found can also be noted if desired.) For example, if you desire to start with John 3:16, then place the reference, Luke 16:19-25 or Hebrews 2:3 beside it. By these two verses place the reference John 1:12, and so on.

You may decide to have two or three "chains" of salvation Scripture passages marked in this manner in your Testament. One chain might be as suggested in our sample Salvation Conversation: John 3:16; Luke 16:19-25; Hebrews 2:3; John 1:12; Revelation 3:20.

Another chain might be "the road to salvation in Romans": Romans 3:23; 6:23; 5:8; 10:9, 10, 13; 8:16.

Still another might be: Romans 3:23; 6:23; 1 John 1:9; John 1:12; Revelation 3:20.

Experienced soul winners will seldom refer to these chains. They will know just what verse to use next in a given conversation and where that verse is found. But nothing will do more to start a new soul winner on the road to experience than securing a Testament and marking it as suggested.

Another helpful technique is to "tab" the pages of the Testament where the references are found using small, transparent Scotch tape tabs. By tabbing the verses, from the top to bottom in sequence on the side of the Testament, the soul winner can quickly find the verses he would like to use.

CHAPTER **9**

THE SOUL WINNER'S FOLLOW-UP ASSIGNMENT

What happens after we have won a soul to Christ? Nature shows us one possibility. The sprouting seed left unprotected soon dies. Eternity will reveal that many who were interested in the kingdom of God, who may even have begun to walk in it, were lost because they were not given proper attention and care.

The new convert must not be expected to stand alone. He must be drawn into the fellowship of the church, where he will receive strength and inspiration from fellow believers. In the activities of the church he will learn to use his own special abilities in service for Christ. He will learn to share salvation with others.

The help given a new convert is part of the follow-up activities necessary in all soul winning. In this chapter we will deal with follow-up as it relates to four distinct facets of soul winning: (1) follow-up of prospects, (2) follow-up of converts, (3) follow-up for enlistment and training, (4) follow-up for worship and work. The first two divisions are concerned with converting and confirming; the last two give attention to involvement and perpetuation.

FOLLOW-UP OF PROSPECTS

Prospects, as the word is used here, means those with whom initial contact has already been made and who are considered likely candidates for conversion. In the broad sense, all unsaved people are prospects for conversion, but you will quickly find that some persons are more likely to respond than others.

DETERMINING WHO ARE PROSPECTS

Some attention has already been given to this in previous chapters. However, our concern here is learning to know how prospects are responding after the first contact has been made.

1. *Interest and need.* Those who are disinterested, deeply entrenched in other religions, antagonistic, self-sufficient, or argumentative are not usually the best prospects. Far more success will be experienced with the interested, the unsatisfied, the openhearted, the needy, the guilt-ridden. Jesus spent little time with the disinterested dwellers at Gadara; but He gave two whole days to the Samaritans of Sychar simply because the Samaritans showed genuine interest.[1] Interest and recognition of need guide our pursuit of prospects.

2. *Inquiry and hunger.* Few are better prospects than those who sincerely inquire and express desire. The inquiring ruler of the Jews, Nicodemus, found Jesus' ready attention. The hungering Gentile, Cornelius, became an easy convert.

3. *Divine discernment.* This is a most important factor in dealing with prospects. While the soul winner should employ his best judgment, he must learn well that there is One who "seeth not as man seeth; for man looketh on the outward appearance, but the

Lord looketh on the heart."[2] No one recognizes prospects as clearly as God and those who know His voice. God knew the Ethiopian eunuch was a prime prospect, and because Philip knew God's voice he "followed him up."

KEEPING OUR PURPOSE CLEAR

A single purpose must motivate the soul winner in his follow-up activity—the same purpose which motivated the Master. His motive is revealed in His words, "For the Son of man is come to seek and to save that which was lost."[3]

As Robert E. Coleman puts it, "His objective was clear. The days of His flesh were but the unfolding in time of the plan of God from the beginning. It was always before His mind. He intended to save out of the world a people for Himself and to build a church of the Spirit which would never perish. . . . His life was ordered by His objective. Everything He did and said was a part of the whole pattern."[4]

Any lesser motive than the Master's is unworthy of the Christian's time and devotion. And, strangely enough, our motives have a way of showing through and even of determining the reaction of those with whom we deal.

MAKING REGULAR CONTACTS

A good prospect may require numerous contacts before his conversion. Persistence pays. A large mail order house has determined that it is a paying proposition to circularize a potential customer over ninety times without a single response. Sometimes we sow; sometimes we reap. Repeated contacts will win people who are not touched in a single visit.

PRAYING AND WORKING TOWARD A DESIRED END

Conversion is the goal; it is a goal reached by the combined efforts of God and man. It is a divine exploit wrought through human instrumentality. Therefore, the soul winner must exercise himself in two directions. He must (1) maintain vital contact with God, and (2) he must make vital and possibly repeated contact with men.

A record of prospects and a prayer list will help the soul winner keep in touch with both man and God. However, the value of a prospect list depends on how it is used. Certainly, a name on a file card is valueless unless it is put to proper use. But a prospect list may serve very well as a reminder. It is too easy to learn of a hungry soul and then to straightway forget him. The prospect list, if properly used, will keep him constantly before us.

The prospect list can also help us be systematic in contacting prospects. It can prevent us from neglecting some, while bestowing more than necessary attention on others.

A prayer request list grows out of the names in the prospect file. The list can be duplicated and distributed to individuals and prayer groups within the church. Perhaps the greatest advantage of the prayer list is the interest it generates in the hearts of those who pray. It is difficult, if not impossible, to pray long for someone without becoming involved in ministering to that individual in other ways.

FOLLOW-UP OF CONVERTS

In the natural, it is the babe who requires the most attention. Neglect, even for a short period, spells almost certain death. So it is with the newly saved. They

are the "lambs," the "little ones," for whom Jesus
showed such great concern and to whom Paul gave
considerable attention. Three factors for successful
follow-up of new converts deserve attention: personnel,
purposes, and special helps.

PERSONNEL

Suitable personnel is a requirement for successful
follow-up. The wrong person can do more harm than
good. The right person can be very helpful to the
new convert. Personnel should be chosen carefully and
trained thoroughly with these qualities in mind:

1. *Spirituality.* The newly saved need spiritual help
most of all. For this reason the spiritually minded and
mature are indispensable to a follow-up program. An
"infant" will be of little help to another "infant."

2. *Appearance.* First impressions are lasting. While
outward appearance may be only skin-deep, the impression it makes often goes much deeper. Follow-up
personnel should be neat, clean, and unoffensive.[5] Ex-
tremes in outward appearance should be avoided in
favor of moderation and modesty.[6]

3. *Adaptability.* The apostle Paul said, "I am made
all things to all men, that I might by all means save
some."[7] Those engaging in follow-up ministry must
be prepared to adapt to a variety of circumstances,
such as wealth, poverty, the educated, the uneducated,
antagonistic relatives, domestic problems, and religious
prejudices.

4. *Responsibility.* There is no more important task
than that which relates to the soul; and since the
souls of men are at stake in follow-up of the newly
saved, only responsible people should be entrusted
with so high an assignment.

In every soul-winning situation, there should be those who are responsible for immediate follow-up. Some use the "big brother" idea to good advantage. In this arrangement, an established Christian becomes responsible for giving regular and careful attention to the newly-won convert until he is able to walk alone.

PURPOSES

Follow-up apart from clearly defined purposes is hardly worthy of the name. But follow-up controlled by Biblical objectives yields high dividends. In Paul's follow-up activities, some of these objectives can be clearly seen: (1) confirmation and exhortation (Acts 14:21, 22); (2) establishment (Romans 1:11); (3) second benefit (2 Corinthians 1:15); (4) establishment and comfort (1 Thessalonians 3:1, 2).

We must determine what objectives we are trying to reach in our follow-up activities. Our objectives give us a measurement of our success.

1. *Encouragement.* Nothing encourages a new convert more than showing personal interest in him. The soul winner whose interest is more than casual and temporary is worth a thousand who make a big splash and then forget the new convert exists.

2. *Fellowship.* The new convert may suddenly find himself cut off from his worldly companions. His usual fellowship with them is over. His chances for being a happy Christian will be greatly increased if ample fellowship is provided. It can be said with certainty that the new convert's future and spiritual stature will be governed largely by the fellowship Christians give him.

"Really," says Robert E. Coleman, "the whole problem of giving personal care to every believer is only resolved in a thorough understanding of the nature and mission of the church. It is well here to observe that the emergence of the church principle around Jesus, whereby one believer was brought into fellowship with all others, was the practice in a large dimension of the same thing He was doing with the twelve. Actually it was the church that was the means of following up all those who followed Him. That is, the group of believers became the body of Christ, and as such ministered to each other individually and collectively.

"Every member of the community of faith had a part to fulfill in this ministry. But this they could only do as they themselves were trained and inspired."[8]

3. *Instruction.* Those engaged in follow-up often have a superb opportunity to lay a firm foundation for the spiritual life of the newly saved. Through informal instruction, the worker can guide the new convert in regular church attendance (Hebrews 10:25), personal testimony (Romans 10:9 and Revelation 12:11), water baptism (Acts 2:38 and 19:4, 5), baptism with the Holy Spirit (Acts 9:2-6), Bible reading (Psalm 1:1), prayer (Matthew 6:6 and James 4:8), and practical Christian living.

SPECIAL HELPS

Follow-up can be made more meaningful if the workers are supplied with helpful items for the new convert. Heading the list of such items is a Bible or New Testament. No newly saved person should be left for long without the Word of God for his own use. Carefully selected literature is also valuable. Include such items as *The Pentecostal Evangel,* a suitable Sunday school quarterly, and pamphlets or tracts especially prepared for new converts. Literature projecting the ministries of the church is also worthwhile.

Follow-up for Enlistment and Training

Conversion is not the end of Christianity; it is the beginning. Each convert must be taught that he has received to share, and to this end he must be enlisted and trained.

enlistment

Blessed is he who winneth souls, but more blessed yet is the person who enlists others in soul winning. Effective enlistment includes: (1) stimulating vision and revealing need, (2) soliciting prayer-concern, (3) demonstrating personal commitment, and (4) projecting the rewards.

1. *Stimulating vision and revealing need.* It is not hard to get people to help win souls when they really recognize the need. When there is no actual war to be fought, our country must resort to every conceivable means of enticement to obtain an adequate supply of men for its armed forces. But let a war emergency arise, and without hesitation thousands are almost instantly ready to enlist. Likewise, when Christians really see the need of lost souls, they will take soul winning seriously.

When Jesus sought to enlist His followers as soul winners, He began very simply. He said to them, "Lift up your eyes, and look on the fields."[9] God does not force a vision of the field upon any. He awaits our cooperation before He imparts vision. You "lift up your eyes"; you "look"—these are His entreaties. Thus, the first step toward enlistment is to gain the gaze of the potential enlistee. In simplest terms, we must direct his attention to the field so ready for reaping.

2. *Soliciting prayer concern.* When men begin to pray about a need, they are likely to become involved in working to answer that need. Vision and recognition of need precede prayer, and prayer precedes personal involvement. Note how Jesus recognized this sequence in Matthew 9:37, 38: "Then saith He unto His disciples, the harvest truly is plenteous, but the labourers are few; Pray ye therefore the Lord of the harvest, that he will send forth labourers into his harvest."

3. *Demonstrating personal commitment to the task.* Jesus had no problem persuading His disciples to join Him in soul winning. The souls of men were more important to Him than material things, and everyone with whom He associated knew it.

One pastor became concerned over the need for contacting the people of his community. He tried various means to get the people of his church involved, with very little response. Then the Lord began to speak to him, indicating that regardless of whether anyone else was willing to get involved, he must personally make an effort to contact the people.

He began by spending several hours each week witnessing in nearby homes and inviting the people to attend services. When he began to report to his congregation on his efforts, he discovered they were gripped and before long a sizable number of his people became involved in similar efforts. His personal involvement produced its own good fruit.

4. *Projecting the rewards.* Jesus said, "I have meat to eat that ye know not of."[10] In this way He revealed the delight and satisfaction He found in winning souls.

Shaka Zulu, of the Zulu tribe, was an African chief

during the time of Napoleon. He ruled as large an area as did the Frenchman, but the dark continent obscured his fame.

He was a military genius beyond his times and trained his men in a new type of warfare. Instead of an exchange of spear-throwing, as was the custom, he equipped his men with short swords and ordered his men not to throw their spears in battle.

Then when the enemy had cast their spears, the order was to keep them and not return them. This disarmed the enemy, and on the command of Shaka, the men would charge and engage the enemy in personal combat. Thrusting the enemy's shields aside with their own, Shaka's men would expose their opponents' left side and with the cry, "Ngahla!" (I have eaten) they would thrust their swords through their victims' hearts.

The death of the enemy was their reward and satisfying "meat." But Jesus spoke of satisfying "meat" of another sort—a soul delivered from death. Then, as if to inspire those whom He sought to enlist, He added, "And he that reapeth receiveth wages, and gathereth fruit unto eternal life."[11] It is in perfect order to stimulate enlistment by projecting the rewards for soul winning.

TRAINING

There is no substitute for on-the-job training in soul winning. "When will the church learn this lesson?" asks Robert E. Coleman. He continues, "Preaching to the masses, although necessary, will never suffice in the work of preparing leaders for evangelism. Nor can occasional prayer meetings and training classes for Christian workers do the job. Building men is not that easy. It requires constant personal attention, much like a father gives to his children. This is something that no organization or class can ever do. The example of Jesus would teach us that it can only be done by persons staying right with those they seek to lead.

"The church obviously has failed at this point, and failed tragically. There is a lot of talk in the church about evangelism and Christian nurture, but little concern for personal association when it becomes evident that such work involves the sacrifice of personal indulgence.

"With such haphazard follow-up of believers, it is no wonder that about half of those who make professions and join the church eventually fall away or lose the glow of a Christian experience, and fewer still grow in sufficient knowledge and grace to be of any real service to the Kingdom. . . . This means that some system must be found whereby every convert is given a Christian friend to follow until such time as he can lead another."[12]

Action-training knows no satisfactory substitute. We tend to become like those with whom we associate, in whatever realm it may be. The new convert can get no better training in soul winning than working by the side of the experienced soul winner. He may at first be only a silent witness—an observer. But let him see the soul winner in action and before long he too will be involved.

He should be encouraged in the early stages to simply give his testimony. Through expressing himself, he will gain strength and confidence. As he developes he should be taught to share the Word of God with others and to "preach" Christ to them.

FOLLOW-UP FOR WORSHIP AND WORK

Soul-winning training is not completed in "six easy lessons" or even in a full-orbed personal worker's course. Actually it is a lifetime matter. Although the new convert should begin his soul-winning efforts without delay after his conversion, it is the church's responsibility to lead him ever onward toward greater fruitfulness.

Soul winners are not born. They are made. There is to be a never-ending making process. Remember Jesus' invitation to Peter and Andrew: "Follow me and I will make you fishers of men."[18] Soul winning is not to be divorced from the church or separated like an orphan child from its mother. There is always danger that we place more emphasis on soul winning than on *making* soul winners. Yet the Biblical emphasis is the reverse of that.

The new convert must be tied into the whole worship and study activity of the church, for it is in this whole process that the body ministers to itself and the "making" occurs. Worship and work must be joined together in a sort of holy union. While worshipers are being developed, soul winners must be being "made." Worship is the heart of man reaching God-ward. Work is the heart of God reaching manward. The church must specialize in both areas and one dare not be overemphasized at the expense of the other. The Early Church was great in both. Her worship was unexcelled; and her work was unparalleled. How is this preparation made?

PREPARATION FOR WORSHIP

A. W. Tozer said, "God saves men to make them worshipers . . . What we are overlooking is that no one can be a worker who is not first a worshiper. Labor that does not spring out of worship is futile and can only be wood, hay and stubble in the day that shall try every man's works.

"It may be set down as an axiom that if we do not worship we cannot work acceptably. The Holy Spirit can work through a worshiping heart and through no other kind. We may go through the motions and delude ourselves by our religious activity, but we are setting ourselves up for a shocking disillusionment some-day."[14]

How are worshipers made? Here are some guidelines to worshiping in spirit and in truth.

1. *Give precedence to the Holy Spirit.* The Holy Spirit is both the instigator and perfecter of worship. Wherever He is duly recognized, received, and heeded, worship will be the norm.[15]

2. *Give priority to the Holy Scriptures.* The Holy Spirit and the Holy Scriptures require each other for complete fulfillment. Worship reaches its highest perfection when it is begotten in the human heart by the Holy Spirit through the Word.

3. *Give prominence to worshipful song.* Song is the sweetest language of the soul and a transcending vehicle for worship. If the church is to develop worshipers, she must make wise and noble use of this means.[16]

4. *Give place to spontaneous praise.* Combine the Holy Spirit and the Holy Scriptures, add to this holy song, and spontaneous praise is inevitable.

PREPARATION FOR WORK

Soul-winning training, although it must be perpetually done, is not limited to a single method. In fact there is room for vast variety. From one viewpoint, virtually all ministry to the church should be aimed at completely furnishing the saints for ministry. However, there are also special means by which the soul winner can be prepared for his work.

1. *Develop a soul-winner's fellowship.* This need not be a formal church gathering, but can be effectively carried on in the homes of those involved. It is simply a coming together of those who have been engaging in soul-winning activity, for the purpose of sharing testimonies, discovering more effective methods, dealing with problems, encouraging each other, and praying together.

2. *Provide special courses for soul winners.* Numerous excellent courses are available for this purpose and others are constantly being developed. Courses covering the broad aspects of soul winning should be offered first. Then as time permits the field may be broadened to meet special needs. For example, it may be discovered that several members of a soul-winning group are experiencing problems in dealing with cultists. A course on the cults would help them.

3. *Set up a soul-winners' library.* Many excellent books are available for the soul winner's encouragment and personal improvement. For a bibliography of suitable books contact the Spiritual Life—Evangelism Coordinator, 1445 Boonville, Springfield, Missouri 65802.

4. *Encourage participation in special soul-winning efforts.* Whenever soul-winning seminars and conferences are conducted in the area, they provide good training for new and seasoned personal soul winners.

The strongest drive to win souls will always be the joy of having helped a sinner become a saint. Involvement—that will keep a person concerned about

the lost and anxious to lead others to the Saviour.
Help the new convert become involved with the soul-
winning activities of your church. He will then catch
the enthusiasm and desire.

CONCLUSION

We often speak of soul winning as a command of
Christ and a responsibility. It is, and these are solemn
obligations for us to consider. But soul winning is also
a thrilling adventure in Christian living. It has the
excitement of faith in action, the warm satisfaction
of helping someone in need.

Opportunities surround us daily, and now we know
how to take advantage of those opportunities. Let us
begin immediately to share our faith, to win to Christ
the waiting, needy multitudes who live and work and
shop and play in our communities and neighborhoods.

FOOTNOTES

PREFACE

[1] John 17:18
[2] John 20:21
[3] Luke 14:22
[4] Acts 5:42
[5] Acts 20:20
[6] Mark 16:15
[7] Acts 1:8

CHAPTER 1

[1] Revelation 5:4, 5
[2] John 1:29
[3] 1 John 2:1, 2
[4] 1 Timothy 2:6; 4:10
[5] Revelation 5:9-13
[6] 1 Timothy 2:4
[7] 2 Peter 3:9
[8] Matthew 28:19
[9] Mark 16:15
[10] Luke 24:47
[11] Romans 2:11
[12] Romans 10:11-13
[13] Revelation 22:17
[14] John 3:18
[15] John 3:36
[16] 2 Thessalonians 1:8
[17] Genesis 28:11, 12
[18] John 1:51
[19] John 3:16; John 10:36
[20] 2 Corinthians 5:19; Romans 6:4
[21] 1 Peter 2:24
[22] John 10:15, 18
[23] Luke 24:46
[24] John 16:8
[25] John 6:44
[26] John 12:32
[27] Acts 1:8
[28] Luke 24:47, 48
[29] Romans 10:14
[30] Matthew 28:19
[31] Acts 10:1-5
[32] 2 Timothy 2:2
[33] John 17:20

CHAPTER 2

[1] Genesis 3:8, 9
[2] Genesis 18:1
[3] Exodus 34:6, 7
[4] Exodus 3:2-4
[5] Exodus 3:9
[6] 1 Samuel 3:7
[7] Isaiah 6:8
[8] John 1:14
[9] John 1:18
[10] Revelation 3:20
[11] John 1:29, 35, 36
[12] John 1:43
[13] John 3:16
[14] John 3:22; 4:2-4
[15] John 4:9
[16] Luke 4:38, 39
[17] Luke 4:40
[18] Luke 5:27-29
[19] Luke 7:36
[20] Luke 19:10
[21] John 5:6
[22] Matthew 9:35
[23] Luke 8:1
[24] Luke 15:2
[25] Matthew 4:18, 19
[26] 1 Peter 2:21

CHAPTER 3

[1] Acts 13:2
[2] Acts 16:25
[3] Mark 16:15
[4] Luke 24:47
[5] Matthew 10:1
[6] Mark 6:7
[7] Mark 16:17, 18
[8] Luke 10:1
[9] Matthew 28:20; Mark 16:20
[10] Matthew 10:14; Luke 10:10-12
[11] Acts 13:46, 51
[12] Acts 19:9
[13] Luke 10:17
[14] Acts 14:27
[15] Acts 21:17-19
[16] Matthew 28:7
[17] John 20:17
[18] Luke 14:23
[19] Acts 8:26
[20] Acts 9:11
[21] Matthew 28:18, 20
[22] Mark 16:15
[23] Luke 24:47
[24] 1 Corinthians 1:21

[25] Titus 1:2, 3
[26] Luke 9:60
[27] Acts 20:7, 9
[28] Luke 3:18; Acts 8:4
[29] Acts 4:2; Colossians 1:28
[30] Matthew 3:1; Acts 8:5
[31] Mark 2:2; Acts 16:6
[32] Mark 2:1, 2
[33] Acts 5:28
[34] Acts 5:42
[35] Acts 8:26-38
[36] Acts 11:18
[37] Acts 10:20
[38] Acts 10:46
[39] Acts 13:2-4
[40] Acts 13:13, 14
[41] Acts 14:1-28
[42] Romans 15:19
[43] 1 Corinthians 15:10
[44] 1 Timothy 1:16
[45] 1 Corinthians 11:1
[46] 1 Corinthians 4:16
[47] Philippians 3:17; 4:9
[48] 1 Thessalonians 1:8
[49] 1 Thessalonians 1:23
[50] Romans 10:18
[51] John T. Sisemore, *The Ministry of Visitation* (Nashville: Broadman Press, 1954), pp. 15, 16.
[52] Earle Cairns, *Christianity Through the Centuries* (Grand Rapids: Zondervan Publishing House, 1954), p. 102.

CHAPTER 4

[1] John 4:35
[2] Matthew 23:37
[3] Romans 1:16
[4] Acts 5:42
[5] Luke 17:16
[6] Acts 1:4, 5
[7] Acts 10:38
[8] Acts 2:1-4
[9] Acts 2:39
[10] Luke 10:17
[11] Acts 14:26, 27

[12] Acts 4:8
[13] Acts 6:10; Acts 13:9
[14] Romans 8:14
[15] Matthew 10: 19, 20
[16] Acts 3:16
[17] Galatians 2:20
[18] 2 Corinthians 3:5
[19] 1 Thessalonians 5:17; Romans 12:12
[20] Acts 3:1
[21] Acts 4:23, 24
[22] Acts 6:4
[23] Acts 13:3
[24] Luke 19:41
[25] Matthew 9:36
[26] 2 Corinthians 2:4
[27] Psalm 42:3
[28] Joel 1:13; 2:17
[29] Ezekiel 9:4-6
[30] Jeremiah 9:1
[31] Daniel 10:2
[32] Nehemiah 1:4
[33] Psalm 126:5, 6
[34] Joshua 1:9
[35] Proverbs 18:24

CHAPTER 6

[1] John 3:1, 2
[2] John 4:4
[3] Mark 6:7; Luke 10: 31
[4] John 4:38
[5] Genesis 3:2
[6] Romans 8:29
[7] 2 Corinthians 3:18
[8] Mark 8:34; 10:32-45
[9] John 14:15; see also John 14:21, 23; 15: 12, 13, 14
[10] Acts 2:1, 4, 14
[11] Acts 4:10
[12] Acts 4:31, 33
[13] 1 Timothy 1:6-8

[14] John 4:38
[15] Mark 6:7; Matthew 10:5; Luke 9:1, 2
[16] Myron S. Augsburger, *Invitation to Discipleship* (Scottdale, Penna: Herald Press, 1964), p. 95.
[17] 1 Corinthians 9:22
[18] Luke 4:42
[19] Luke 24; John 20; John 21; Matthew 28
[20] Mark 10
[21] Luke 10
[22] John 4
[23] 2 Corinthians 5:17

CHAPTER 8

[1] Acts 20:21
[2] Luke 13:3
[3] 1 John 1:9
[4] Ephesians 2:8
[5] Romans 3:25
[6] Romans 5:1
[7] Hebrews 6:11
[8] Acts 8:37
[9] Hebrews 11:6
[10] Romans 5:8, 9
[11] Romans 10:10, 11
[12] Matthew 12:29
[13] John 1:29, 30
[14] John 3:30
[15] 1 Corinthians 3:27
[16] Matthew 13:23
[17] D. V. Hurst, *Ye Shall Be Witnesses* (Springfield, Mo.: Gospel Publishing House, 1952), p. 135
[18] Romans 11:17
[19] Romans 8:16
[20] Jude 20

[21] Acts 2:42
[22] John 8:31
[23] Revelation 3:10

CHAPTER 9

[1] Luke 8:37; John 4:40
[2] 1 Samuel 16:7
[3] Luke 19:10
[4] Robert E. Coleman, *The Master Plan of Evangelism* (New Jersey: Fleming H. Revell Co., 1963) pp. 17, 18
[5] 2 Corinthians 6:3
[6] Philippians 4:5; 1 Timothy 2:9
[7] 1 Corinthians 9:22
[8] Robert E. Coleman, *The Master Plan of Evangelism*, pp. 46, 47
[9] John 4:35
[10] John 4:32
[11] John 4:36
[12] Robert E. Coleman, *The Master Plan of Evangelism*, pp. 47, 48
[13] Matthew 4:19
[14] A. W. Tozer, *Born After Midnight* (Harrisburg, Pa.: Christian Publications Inc., 1959) pp. 125, 126
[15] 1 Thessalonians 1:18; John 4:23, 24; Acts 2:11; 10:46
[16] 2 Chronicles 4:12-14; Ephesians 5:19; Colossians 3:16